The
Selected
*Poems of* Nikki
Giovanni

# Books by Nikki Giovanni

POETRY

*Black Feeling Black Talk/Black Judgement*
*Re: Creation*
*My House*
*The Women and the Men*
*Cotton Candy On A Rainy Day*
*Those Who Ride the Night Winds*

PROSE

*Gemini: An Extended Autobiographical Statement on My First Twenty-Five Years of Being a Black Poet*
*A Dialogue: James Baldwin and Nikki Giovanni*
*A Poetic Equation: Conversations Between Nikki Giovanni and Margaret Walker*
*Sacred Cows . . . and Other Edibles*
*Racism 101*

EDITED BY NIKKI GIOVANNI

*Night Comes Softly: Anthology of Black Female Voices*
*Appalachian Elders: A Warm Hearth Sampler*
*Grand Mothers: A Multicultural Anthology of Poems, Reminiscences, and Short Stories About the Keepers of Our Traditions*
*Shimmy Shimmy Shimmy Like My Sister Kate*

FOR CHILDREN

*Spin a Soft Black Song*
*Vacation Time: Poems for Children*
*Ego Tripping and Other Poems for Young People*
*Knoxville, Tennessee*
*The Geni in the Jar*
*. . . And Peppermint Dreams*
*Legacies*

# The Selected

*Poems of* Nikki Giovanni

William Morrow and Company, Inc.

New York

The chronology is from *Conversations with Nikki Giovanni*, edited by Virginia C.
Fowler, copyright © 1992 by University Press of Mississippi. Reprinted by
permission of Virginia C. Fowler and University Press of Mississippi. The
chronology was updated in 1995 by Virginia C. Fowler.

Library of Congress Cataloging-in-Publication Data

Giovanni, Nikki.
    [Poems. Selections]
    The selected poems of Nikki Giovanni.
        p.  cm.
    ISBN 0–688–14047–5
    1. Women—United States—Poetry.   2. Afro-American women—Poetry.
3. Afro-Americans—Poetry.   I. Title.
    PS3557.0I55A6   1996
    811'.54—dc20                                                    95–31646
                                                                       CIP

Printed in the United States of America


                            18 19 20

BOOK DESIGN BY LINDA KOCUR

*The nature of this art is lonely: the writer puts forth a vision and hopes some other person will carry it forward; yet writers, like all people, need other humans. I have been fortunate that Gloria Haffer is my friend and attorney. I am even luckier that as my friend she is always on my side but as my attorney she stands solidly behind her own judgment. The twenty years she has been a force in my life and career have been good, fun, and productive and my only hope is that we will go through the next twenty or so years together.*

# Contents

**The Women and the Men**

**Cotton Candy On A Rainy Day**

**Those Who Ride the Night Winds**

# Foreword

"We cannot possibly leave it to history as a discipline," Nikki Giovanni writes in an essay, "nor to sociology nor science nor economics to tell the story of our people."[1] Instead, she continues, that story must be told by writers. To read through this volume of Giovanni's poetry is indeed to read "the story" of the last twenty-five years of American life, as that life has been lived, observed, and reflected about by a racially conscious Black woman. The "Black is beautiful" slogan of the 1960s is given joyous and vivid embodiment in a poem like "Beautiful Black Men," for example, which celebrates the arrogant new strut of Black men "walking down the street." At the same time, we are reminded by a work like "Woman Poem" that the new racial pride was not always as liberating for Black women as it was for Black men because "it's a sex object if you're pretty/and no love/ or love and no sex if you're fat/get back fat black woman be a mother/grandmother strong thing but not woman."

The rage felt by so many Black Americans at America's persistent and destructive racism is registered in poems like the fine "Great Pax Whitie," which includes allusions to the assassinations of John F. Kennedy and Malcolm X. The topicality of many of Giovanni's poems grounds them in the historical moment in which they were written, even as the emotional and intellectual responses to specific events transcend the particular and become universal. Although such topicality is frequently disparaged by literary critics, it is central to Giovanni's conception of poetry and the poet. "Poetry," she has written, "is but a reflection of the moment. The universal comes from the particular" (*Sacred Cows*, p. 57). Further, she has stated that "I have even gone so far as to think one of the duties of this profession is to be topical, to try to say something about the times in which we are living and how we both view and evaluate them" (*Sacred Cows*, pp. 32–33). This conception of the poet and poetry is consistent with the aesthetic

[1] *Sacred Cows . . . and Other Edibles* (New York: William Morrow, 1988), p. 61; hereafter cited in text.

theories of the Black Arts Movement, from which Giovanni was one of the most popular and controversial young writers to emerge; these writers sought to create, in the words of Amiri Baraka, "an art that would actually reflect black life and its history and legacy of resistance and struggle!"[2]

Giovanni herself connects the importance of topicality in poetry to the tradition of the African *griot;* like the *griots,* she writes, Black American poets "have traveled the length and breadth of the planet singing our song of the news of the day, trying to bring people closer to the truth" (*Sacred Cows,* pp. 33–34). Her poems thus often speak directly about specific events or people, giving expression to the emotions they provoke and disclosing the realities and truths that underlie them—as she sees them. Giovanni does not believe, however, that the poet is a "god," or that the poet has visionary powers beyond those of people who are not poets or writers. She also denies the power of poetry to change the world; as she has stated, "I don't think that writers ever changed the mind of anybody. I think we always preach to the saved."[3] What, then, is poetry? And why does she write it?

The answers to those questions are inextricably tied to Giovanni's consciousness of her identity as a Black American and to her recognition of the struggle of Black Americans to find a voice that would express themselves and their realities: "The African slave bereft of his gods, his language, his drums searched his heart for a new voice. Under sun and lash the African sought meaning in life on earth and the possibility of life hereafter. They shuffled their feet, clapped their hands, gathered a collective audible breath to release the rhythms of the heart. We affirmed in those dark days of chattel through the White Knights of Emancipation that all we had was a human voice to guide us and a human voice to answer the call" (*Sacred Cows,* p. 52). Giovanni's poetry (as well as her prose) represents her own efforts to give voice to her vision of truth and reality as honestly as she can because, she has said, "the only thing you bring . . . is your honesty."[4] The "truth" her

[2]Amiri Baraka, "Foreword: The Wailer," in *Visions of A Liberated Future: Black Arts Movement Writings by Larry Neal,* ed. Michael Schwartz (New York: Thunder's Mouth Press, 1989), p. x.

[3]Arlene Elder, "A MELUS Interview: Nikki Giovanni," *MELUS* 9 (Winter 1982): 61–75; reprinted in *Conversations with Nikki Giovanni,* ed. Virginia C. Fowler (Jackson: University Press of Mississippi, 1992), p. 126.

[4]Ibid., p. 128.

poetry speaks, then, is always the truth as she honestly sees it, and this honesty of expression is what, for her, determines that her poetry is, in fact, art: "I like to think that if truth has any bearing on art, my poetry and prose is art because it's truthful." (*Sacred Cows*, p. 66). Articulating through poetry her vision of reality is the equivalent of the slaves' recognition that their survival depended on their finding "a human voice to guide us and a human voice to answer the call." The loneliness inherent in the human condition is, Giovanni has said, assuaged by art, for "we are less lonely when we connect," and "Art is a connection. I like being a link. I hope the chain will hold" (*Sacred Cows*, p. 58).

The development of a unique and distinctive *voice* has been perhaps the single most important achievement of Giovanni's career. Although even the most superficial perusal of this volume will reveal many changes in tone, in ideas, and in subjects throughout Giovanni's writing career, what remains consistent— even while we watch it grow in maturity and confidence—is the voice speaking to us from the page. Many readers of Giovanni's poetry actually come to her written work after having heard her read from it. And in part because Giovanni has literally taken her poetry "to the people" through hundreds of public lectures and readings over the last twenty-five years, her spoken voice is immediately recognizable by countless people. Seeking to simulate spoken language, the poetry itself possesses distinctive oral qualities. Because it is always intended to be read aloud, its full impact can frequently be felt only through hearing it. In her poetry Giovanni attempts to continue African and African-American oral traditions, and she seems in many ways to have less reverence for the written word than for the spoken.

Often, for example, Giovanni's poetry draws our attention to the limitations and artificiality of language and of language shaped into what we call "art." In "My House," for example, the speaker repeatedly asks us "does this really sound/like a silly poem?" until she finally and explicitly asserts that "english isn't a good language/to express emotion through/mostly i imagine because people/try to speak english instead/of trying to speak through it." Written language, the poem suggests, becomes a barrier to expression and understanding when we treat it as an end in itself rather than as a means to an end. The aesthetic assumption underlying this conception of language is obviously far removed from notions of "art for art's sake." Unless it is connected to the realities of life, art, for Giovanni, lacks both meaning and value.

One of Giovanni's most explicit, though lighthearted, treatments of the subject of language and poetry is found, appropriately, in "A Poem for langston hughes." This playful love poem represents one of the few instances in her poetry in which Giovanni consciously attempts to employ the style of another writer. The poem's rhythms, rhyme, and images collectively evoke the essence of Langston Hughes, whose poetry and career have significantly influenced Giovanni's own. Drawing almost nonsensically on many of the formal elements of poetry, the speaker of the poem states:

> *metaphor has its point of view*
> *allusions and illusion . . . too*

> *meter . . . verse . . . classical . . . free*
> *poems are what you do to me*

Poetry, Giovanni here suggests, cannot be reduced to its component parts or rhetorical devices, for poetry is not removed from life but expressive and experiential.

Giovanni's desire, as she states it metaphorically at the end of "Cotton Candy On A Rainy Day," is "To put a three-dimensional picture / On a one-dimensional surface." As a poet who equates the survival of her people with their ability to use the only thing left them, their "human voice," Giovanni must rely on language to create written poems with the immediacy and impact of the spoken word, poems that, like such Black musical forms as the spirituals, the blues, and jazz, communicate directly to a reader/ listener. Thus, she has said that she does not polish or revise the individual words or lines of a poem, but instead will rework the entire poem, for "a poem is a way of capturing a moment. . . . A poem's got to be a single stroke, and I make it the best I can because it's going to live. I feel if only one thing of mine is to survive, it's at least got to be an accurate picture of what I saw. I want my camera and film to record what my eye and my heart saw."[5] The poem is, in many ways, a kind of *gestalt*.

Giovanni frequently writes as though she wishes to distinguish her own poems from the artifice we might normally associate with poetry. Because she sees poetry as "the culture of a people,"[6] she seems to believe that it has an urgency and significance we are not accustomed to expecting from it. Her most recently published poem, which actually opens this volume, provides a good example of Giovanni's strategy of insisting that we see the "single stroke" of meaning. Her strategy in "Stardate Number 18628.190," a poem written for the twenty-fifth anniversary issue of *Essence* magazine, is to repeat, in three of the poem's five stanzas, that what we are reading is not art, but something else. The poem opens and closes, in fact, with the assertion that "This is not a poem." What, then, is it? The entire piece endeavors to identify and represent itself as the Black women whom it in fact celebrates. It accumulates images evocative of the many everyday activities, extraordinary accomplishments, and modes of being of Black women, "the Daughters of the Diaspora." These Daughters have given not a "poem" but "a summer quilt," a metaphor used by Giovanni elsewhere, as well as by numerous contemporary women writers. In "Stardate," Giovanni employs the quilt as a metaphor of family history and family love; the pieces of the quilt are scraps of cloth, each of which reminds the speaker of an event and a person in her family's history, including "grandmother's wedding dress," "grandpappa's favorite Sunday tie," "the baby who died," and Mommy's pneumonia. An appropriate symbol of the transformative powers by which Black Americans have resisted the oppression enacted upon them, the quilt represents the Black woman's creation of beauty out of discarded, worthless bits of material. Even more, however, the history evoked by the quilt and the love and human connection found in that history are what distinguish the quilt from "art": "This does not hang from museum walls...nor will it sell for thousands...This is here to keep me warm." Unlike the "art" collected in museums, which

---

[5]Claudia Tate, *Black Women Writers At Work* (New York: Continuum, 1983); reprinted in Fowler, *Conversations with Nikki Giovanni*, p. 146.

[6]Nikki Giovanni, *Gemini: An Extended Autobiographical Statement on My First Twenty-Five Years of Being a Black Poet* (1971; reprint, New York: Penguin, 1985), p. 95.

may have great monetary value but is, the lines imply, cold and sterile, the quilt's value is based on its warming, life-sustaining, and life-nurturing powers.

The opening words of the third stanza offer a variation on the assertion that "This is not a poem." Beginning with the claim that "This is not a sonnet," the third stanza delineates the music created and sung by Black women, from the spirituals to rap. Significantly, the stanza ends with the reiterated denial that it is a sonnet and the counterclaim that it is instead "the truth of the beauty that the only authentic voice of Planet Earth comes from the black soil . . . tilled and mined . . . by the Daughters of the Diaspora." Perhaps because the sonnet is frequently regarded in Western literary tradition as one of the most elegant poetic forms, mastery of which is often expected of aspiring writers, Giovanni seizes on it in order to juxtapose its artifice to the authenticity of the Black woman's voice. What constitute the "authenticity" of that voice, the poem suggests, are the comfort, support, celebration, encouragement, unselfishness, and prayerfulness that it has lifted itself to speak and sing. In other words, authenticity is a function of human conduct, of ethical behavior. The Black woman's voice is authentic because, as the poem concludes, the Black woman has made "the world a hopeful . . . loving place." Such authenticity of voice is for Giovanni clearly superior to the aesthetic form in which that voice might cast its words. Further, while the sonnet may be a poetic form prized in Western literary traditions, it is not a form capable of expressing Black realities; the Black woman's "authentic" voice has created its own forms through which to sing and speak.

Giovanni's insistence that aesthetic value emerges from and is dependent upon moral value surfaces not only in this, her most recent poem, but in the poems throughout this volume. It is a corollary to her equally consistent belief that the poet writes not from experience but from empathy: "You try as a writer to put yourself into the other person's position. Empathy. Empathy is everything because we can't experience everything. Experience is important, but empathy is the key."[7] Many of Giovanni's po-

[7]Virginia C. Fowler, "An Interview with Nikki Giovanni" in Fowler, *Conversations with Nikki Giovanni*, p. 202.

ems, both early and more recent, make obvious use of empathy, including such pieces as "Poem For Aretha," "Poem For A Lady Whose Voice I Like," "Poem of Angela Yvonne Davis," and "Linkage." But for Giovanni, empathy is not simply a tool for poetically appropriating lives and experiences removed from the world inhabited by the poet; on the contrary, empathy is key to human life and understanding because it is key to human connection (one of the primary purposes of art as she sees it). Empathy enables us to collapse the dualistic structures that polarize our world into "us" and "them." Not surprisingly, many of Giovanni's poems attribute a powerful capacity for empathy to Black women, who "wipe away our own grief... to give comfort to those beyond comfort" ("Hands: For Mother's Day"). The Black woman's unselfish willingness to empathize with others constitutes one of the sources of her authenticity of voice.

As one reads through the poems in this volume, one cannot avoid recognizing that race and gender are inextricably intertwined constituents of Giovanni's thematic concerns. The significance of individual women in the poet's life is evident from the outset of her career—teachers, friends, her mother, and her grandmother are represented in her poems as crucial to her sense of self and well-being. In later poems, especially in those from the *My House* forward, Giovanni demonstrates increasing awareness of the extent to which gender is a problematic component of identity for women. As she says in "A Poem Off Center," "maybe i shouldn't feel sorry / for myself / but the more i understand women / the more i do." Even Giovanni's early militant poems remark the subordinate role women were expected to play in the "revolution." Other early poems take note of the sexist treatment to which the successful Black woman is apt to be subjected by the Black man. In "Poem For A Lady Whose Voice I Like," for example, the male speaker attributes Lena Horne's success to her physical attractiveness and the attention bestowed on her by white people, rather than to her abilities and talent as a singer; his final exasperated charge is that "you pretty full of yourself ain't chu," to which she replies, "show me someone not full of herself / and i'll show you an empty person."

Countless poems play variations on this theme, reiterating the idea that the position women are expected to occupy—solely because of their gender—leaves them "empty" in one way or another. Expected to "sit and wait / cause i'm a woman" ("All I Gotta Do"), women live in a world

| | |
|---|---|
| *made up of baby clothes* | *to be washed* |
| *food* | *to be cooked* |
| *lullabies* | *to be sung* |
| *smiles* | *to be glowed* |
| *hair* | *to be plaited* |
| *ribbons* | *to be bowed* |
| *coffee* | *to be drunk* |
| *books* | *to be read* |
| *tears* | *to be cried* |
| *loneliness* | *to be borne* |
| | "[Untitled]" |

Expected to devote their lives to the needs of others, women do not necessarily receive any gratitude for such devotion, but may actually be punished for it. As Giovanni says in "Boxes,"

> everybody says how strong
> i am
>
> only black women
> and white men
> are truly free
> they say
>
> it's not difficult to see
> how stupid they are
>
> i would not reject
> my strength
> though its source
> is not choice
> but responsibility

Variations on the idea expressed in the final stanza may be found frequently in Giovanni's poetry.

While many of Giovanni's poems explore and describe women's lives, others celebrate women—Black women in particular—as a way of providing an antidote to the slurs so often cast upon them. None offers a more audacious celebration than the enormously popular "Ego Tripping (there may be a reason why)." Without question one of the most powerful celebrations of the Black woman ever written, the poem attributes to her the creation of all the great civilizations of the world. Far from being bound to a narrow and confined existence, the speaker asserts, in the poem's famous concluding words, that "I . . . can fly / like a bird in the sky . . . ." Although "Ego Tripping" accumulates outrageous claims to power ("the filings from my fingernails are / semi-precious jewels," "The hair from my head thinned and gold was laid / across three continents"), it also accurately reflects Giovanni's frankly chauvinistic belief that whatever good we find in our world is attributable to the Black woman. Characteristically, in this poem and many others (as well as in her prose), Giovanni urges that we not be ashamed of an aspect of identity over which we have no control—in this case, gender—just because the world in which we live uses it as a basis for oppression. Although she does not deny the reality of the oppression, she rejects the notion that the victim is responsible for her own oppression. Instead, in what is a frequent gesture, she embraces her gender and her race, and, in poems like "Ego Tripping," offers her own definition and description of the Black woman. She once commented, in fact, that "Ego Tripping" was written in opposition to the gender roles typically taught to little girls; it "was really written for little girls. . . . I really got tired of hearing all of the little girls' games, such as Little Sally Walker."[8]

The speaker in "Poem (For Nina)" similarly emphasizes the importance of embracing her racial identity. If the white world cannot see beyond the color of her skin, and tries to oppress her because of it, then she will embrace in order to celebrate that component of her identity:

[8]Barbara Reynolds, *And Still We Rise: Interviews with 50 Black Role Models* (Washington: Gannett New Media Services, 1988), p. 94.

*if i am imprisoned in my skin let it be a dark world*
*with a deep bass walking a witch doctor to me for spiritual*
*consultation*
*let my world be defined by my skin and the color of my*
    *people*
*for we        spirit to spirit        will embrace*
*this world*

The centrality of race and gender in Giovanni's poetry is emphasized by the poems used to frame the present volume. All of the poems in the volume appear in the order of original composition and/or publication except for the two framing poems. We have already seen the poet's celebration of Black women in "Stardate," which opens the volume. Closing the volume and completing the frame around twenty-five years of work is the powerful "But Since You Finally Asked," which was written to commemorate the tenth anniversary of the slave memorial at Mount Vernon. The initial public reading of this poem at the Mount Vernon ceremony was accompanied by a deluge of rain, and to the participants gathered on the slope overlooking the Potomac River nature itself seemed to join in mourning the "many thousand gone." Giovanni's poem recounts the history of African people brought to America in chains, who were never "asked . . . what we thought of Jamestown," never told " 'Welcome' . . . 'You're Home' ." The poem juxtaposes the ideals expressed in the Declaration of Independence and the Constitution to the realities of life for Black Americans, the only Americans, the poem suggests, who have actually believed in and tried to practice those ideals—which were never intended to include them. Brutally enslaved, denied their humanity, erased from history, Black Americans "didn't write a constitution . . . we live one." Echoing words from the Negro National Anthem ("Lift Every Voice and Sing"), Giovanni concludes the poem with a celebration of the courage, integrity, and generosity of her people.

The two poems that frame this selection of Giovanni's poetry reveal how and why she continues in the 1990s to be a "poet of the people." Unlike many volumes of "selected poetry," this one was not necessitated by the lack of availability which so often occurs as books go out of print. On the contrary, each of the nine volumes of poetry written by Nikki Giovanni over the past twenty-five years has remained continuously in print since its original publication date. This remarkable fact points to the clear and uncontested place Giovanni has earned in the hearts and minds of countless readers, just as the frequency with which her poems are anthologized points to her secure place in literary history. To borrow from her own words in "Stardate," we might well say that this is not a volume of poems but "a celebration of the road we have traveled . . . [and] a prayer . . . for the roads yet to come!"

—VIRGINIA C. FOWLER
July 1995

# Chronology

1943      Yolande Cornelia Giovanni, Jr., born in Knoxville, Tennessee on 7 June, the second child of Yolande and Jones Giovanni. The family moves to Cincinnati, Ohio, in August, but continues to make frequent visits to Knoxville, home of NG's maternal grandparents, Emma Louvenia and John Brown Watson.

1957      NG moves to Knoxville to live with her maternal grandparents. She attends Austin High School, where she comes under the influence of Alfredda Delaney, her English teacher, and Emma Stokes, her French teacher; with NG's grandmother Louvenia, these two teachers were among the most important influences on NG's life.

1960–63      NG leaves high school at the end of her junior year to enroll in Fisk University as an early entrant. She comes into immediate conflict with Fisk's dean of women, Ann Cheatam, and is expelled from Fisk in February, at the end of the first semester, for having visited her grandparents in Knoxville over Thanksgiving without having received the required permission. Her grandfather Watson dies that April. NG moves back to Cincinnati, where she lives with her parents, works at Walgreen's, and occasionally enrolls in classes at the University of Cincinnati. She also becomes a primary caretaker of her nephew, Christopher, who was temporarily living with her parents.

1964–66      NG returns to Fisk University in the fall of 1964, where her old enemy Dean Cheatam has been replaced by Blanche McConnell Cowan, who quickly becomes an important friend and mentor. NG majors in history, edits a student literary/political journal, and reestablishes the Fisk chapter of the Student Nonviolent Coordinating Committee, which had been banned several years earlier. NG begins to look more seriously at writing and studies with John O. Killens. She meets some of the important figures of the Black Arts Movement through Killens's Writers Workshops, including LeRoi Jones. NG completes her undergraduate coursework in December.

1967     NG moves back to Cincinnati, but lives in her own apartment. On 4 February, she is awarded her B.A. in history, with honors. Her grandmother Louvenia, having lost her home to urban "progress," dies a month later on 8 March. NG works on the poems that will make up her first volume, *Black Feeling, Black Talk;* becomes managing editor of a local revolutionary publication, *Conversation;* and organizes Cincinnati's first Black Arts Festival. In May she attends the Detroit Conference of Unity and Art, where she meets H. Rap Brown and other movement leaders. In the fall, she moves to Wilmington, Delaware, works at the People's Settlement House, and, with the assistance of a Ford Foundation fellowship, begins graduate studies at the University of Pennsylvania's School of Social Work.

1968     NG drops out of graduate school and writes most of the poems that will later be collected in her second volume, *Black Judgement.* On 4 April she leaves Wilmington before the National Guard has sealed it and drives to Atlanta for the funeral of Martin Luther King, Jr. In the summer NG moves to New York City, and in the fall she enters the School of Fine Arts of Columbia University, where she is told that she cannot write; she resigns without receiving an M.F.A. in creative writing. At the end of the year, she borrows the money to publish her first volume, *Black Feeling, Black Talk.*

| 1969 | NG teaches at Queens College. She persuades Harold Logan, manager of Birdland, to allow her to have a book party at the club. She works hard to promote the party, which draws an enormous crowd. The line waiting to get in is so long that reporters from *The New York Times*, whose offices are nearby, become interested and, discovering that it is a line for a poetry reading, write a story with photographs and feature it on the front page of the metro section. The publicity generated helps NG to sell 10,000 copies of *Black Feeling, Black Talk* over the next eight months. She receives a grant from the Harlem Council of the Arts, with which she publishes her second volume of poetry, *Black Judgement*. On 31 August, while visiting her parents in Cincinnati for the Labor Day weekend, she gives birth to her only child, Thomas Watson Giovanni. That fall, she begins teaching at Rutgers University. |
|---|---|
| 1970 | NG establishes NikTom, Ltd. She edits and publishes *Night Comes Softly*, one of the first anthologies of poetry by black women. William Morrow publishes NG's first two volumes of poetry under the title *Black Feeling Black Talk/Black Judgement*. Broadside Press, which had distributed the original editions of NG's first two volumes of poetry, publishes *Re: Creation*. NG writes and sells as a broadside "Poem of Angela Yvonne Davis." |
| 1971 | NG makes frequent appearances on the television program *Soul!*, including an appearance in January with Lena Horne. In January *Contact Magazine* names NG Best Poet in its slate of annual awards. NG publishes *Gemini* and *Spin a Soft Black Song*. *Mademoiselle* magazine gives her its "Highest Achievement Award." In July, NG reads her poetry with the gospel music of the New York Community Choir in a free concert at Canaan Baptist Church in Harlem before a crowd of one thousand five hundred; the con- |

cert introduces the album *Truth Is On Its Way*, which was an overnight success. NG learns of the album's success while she is traveling in Africa during the summer. In November, she travels to London to tape the video with James Baldwin that was aired in the United States on 15 December and 22 December; the transcript of the video is published the following year as *A Dialogue: James Baldwin and Nikki Giovanni*. NG falls ill from exhaustion after her return to the United States.

1972    *Truth Is On Its Way* receives N.A.T.R.A.'s Award for Best Spoken Word Album. NG gives a poetry reading at Lincoln Center. She publishes *My House* and *A Dialogue: James Baldwin and Nikki Giovanni*. In November, NG visits with Margaret Walker in Jackson, Mississippi, and the two writers begin working on their dialogue. From 1972 until 1980, NG helps finance, serves as an editorial consultant for, and contributes regular columns to *Encore*, later renamed *Encore American & Worldwide News*, a publishing venture begun by the journalist Ida Lewis, a close friend.

1973    NG meets with Margaret Walker in Washington, D.C., to finish the taping of their dialogue. On 14 May, NG receives one of eight Women of the Year Awards from the *Ladies' Home Journal*; the awards ceremony, held at Washington's Kennedy Center, is aired on nationwide television. NG is criticized by some black leaders for accepting this award. On 21 June, NG gives a poetry recital to celebrate her thirtieth birthday at New York's Philharmonic Hall. She travels in the fall to Africa, on a lecture tour sponsored by the State Department; she visits Ghana, Swaziland, Lesotho, Botswana, Zambia, Tanzania, Kenya, and Nigeria. She is given Life Membership and Scroll by the National Council of Negro Women. The American Library Association names *My House* one of the best books of 1973. NG publishes *Ego Tripping and Other Poems for Young Readers* and releases the album *Like A Ripple On A Pond*.

1974 NG becomes the youngest woman to receive an Honorary Doctorate of Humanities from Wilberforce University, the nation's oldest black college. She publishes *A Poetic Equation: Conversations Between Nikki Giovanni and Margaret Walker*.

1975–78 NG continues to support herself and her son through her writing and frequent lecture/poetry readings. In some years, she makes as many as two hundred personal appearances. She continues to publish and to receive honors and awards. In 1975, she publishes *The Women and the Men* and releases the album *The Way I Feel*. In 1976, she receives an Honorary Doctorate of Literature from Ripon University, and releases two albums, *Legacies* and *The Reason I Like Chocolate*. In 1977 she receives an Honorary Doctorate of Literature from the University of Maryland and in 1978 an Honorary Doctorate of Literature from Smith College. In 1978 she also publishes *Cotton Candy On A Rainy Day* and releases an album of the same title. NG's father has a stroke and is subsequently discovered to have cancer; as a result, NG and her son move back to her parents' home in Cincinnati.

1979–82 NG assumes primary financial responsibility for her parents. She helps care for her father and also maintains a heavy speaking schedule. In 1979, NG publishes *Vacation Time* and is named an Honorary Commissioner for the President's Commission on the International Year of the Child. Her father dies on 8 June 1982, the day after NG's thirty-ninth birthday.

1983–87 NG and her son continue to make their home with her mother. NG is named YWCA Woman of the Year by the Cincinnati chapter of the YWCA. She publishes *Those Who Ride the Night Winds* in 1983. Over the next several years, she returns occasionally to teaching: she is a Visiting Professor of English at Ohio State University in 1984–85 and Professor of Creative Writing at Mount Saint Joseph's College in 1985–87. In 1984, her disagreement with the strategy of boycotting South Africa leads to false accusations against her and blacklisting of her by TransAfrica; she also receives bomb and death threats. In 1985 she makes a European lecture tour for the U.S.I.A.; receives an Honorary Doctorate of Human Letters from the College of Mount Saint Joseph; is named to the Ohio Women's Hall of Fame; and is named Outstanding Woman of Tennessee. In 1986, she receives the Cincinnati *Post*'s Post-Corbett Award and is Duncanson Artist-in-Residence at the Taft Museum in Cincinnati.

1987–92 In 1987, NG accepts a visiting professorship at Virginia Polytechnic Institute and State University, in Blacksburg, Virginia, and in 1989 she agrees to a permanent position. Her mother moves to live with NG's sister in California, and NG establishes permanent residence in Virginia. In 1987, PBS produces a film about her life, *Spirit to Spirit: The Poetry of Nikki Giovanni*. In 1988, NG publishes *Sacred Cows . . . and Other Edibles*, which receives the Ohioana Library Award. *Vacation Time* receives the Children's Reading Roundtable of Chicago Award. In 1988, NG receives an Honorary Doctorate of Humanities from Fisk University, and in 1991 she is awarded an Honorary Doctorate of Humane Letters from Indiana University. In 1991, she was the featured poet of the Utrecht Literary Festival, in Holland. In 1992, she receives an Honorary Doctorate of Humane Letters from Otterbein College.

1993 NG continues to serve on the board of the Virginia Foundation for the Humanities (first appointed in

1991). She receives an Honorary Doctorate of Fine Arts from Rockhurst College and an Honorary Doctorate of Humane Letters from Widener University. During the summer, she is the Hill Visiting Professor at the University of Minnesota. NG writes and presents on 18 September the poem "But Since You Finally Asked" to commemorate the tenth Anniversary Slave Memorial Wreath-Laying at Mount Vernon. She publishes the twentieth-anniversary edition of *Ego Tripping and Other Poems for Young People*, which includes additional new poems.

1994   NG publishes *Racism 101*, a collection of essays, *Knoxville, Tennessee*, an illustrated children's book, and *Grand Mothers: A Multicultural Anthology of Poems, Reminiscences, and Short Stories About the Keepers of Our Traditions*. NG's son, Thomas, graduates magna cum laude from Morehouse College. NG's mother and sister move from California to Virginia. NG receives the Tennessee Writer's Award from *The Nashville Banner*.

1995   NG undergoes successful surgery for lung cancer. During her convalescence, she works on several new books, including a Harlem Renaissance reader and her own *Selected Poems*. She receives an Honorary Doctorate of Literature from Albright College and an Honorary Doctorate of Humane Letters from Cabrini College. NG serves as writer-in-residence for the National Book Foundation's Family Literacy Program at the Family Academy in Harlem and writes "Stardate Number 18628.190," a poem celebrating black women, for the twenty-fifth anniversary issue of *Essence* magazine (published under the title "Light the Candles").

# Stardate Number 18628.190*

This is not a poem . . . this is hot chocolate at the beginning of Spring . . . topped with hand whipped double cream . . . a splash of brandy to give it sass . . . and just a little cinnamon to give it class . . . This is not a poem

This is a summer quilt . . . log cabin pattern . . . see the corner piece . . . that was grandmother's wedding dress . . . that was grandpappa's favorite Sunday tie . . . that white strip there . . . is the baby who died . . . Mommy had pneumonia so that red flannel shows the healing . . . This does not hang from museum walls . . . nor will it sell for thousands . . . This is here to keep me warm

This is not a sonnet . . . though it will sing . . . Precious Lord . . . take my hand . . . Amazing Grace . . . how sweet the sound . . . Go down, Moses . . . Way down to the past . . . Way up to the future . . . It will swell with the voice of Marion Anderson . . . lilt on the arias of Leontyne . . . dance on the trilling of Battle . . . do the dirty dirty with Bessie . . . moan with Dinah Washington . . . rock and roll through the Sixties . . . rap its way into the Nineties . . . and go on out into Space with Etta James saying At Last . . . No, this is not a sonnet . . . but the truth of the beauty that the only authentic voice of Planet Earth comes from the black soil . . . tilled and mined . . . by the Daughters of the Diaspora

This is a rocking chair . . . rock me gently in the bosom of Abraham . . . This is a bus seat: No, I'm not going to move today . . . This is a porch . . . where they sat spitting at fireflies . . . telling young Alex the story of The African . . . This is a hook rug . . . to cover a dirt floor . . . This is an iron pot . . . with the left over vegetables . . . making a slow cooking soup . . . This is pork . . . simmering chitterlings . . . surprising everybody with our ability to make a way . . . out of no way . . . This is not rest when we are weary . . . nor comfort when we are sad . . . It is laughter . . . when we are in pain . . . It

*Written for *Essence* magazine's 25th Anniversary Issue.

is "N'mind" when we are confused . . . It is "Keep climbing, chile" when the road takes the unfair turn . . . It is "Don't let nobody turn you round" . . . when our way is dark . . . It is the faith of our Mothers . . . who plaited our hair . . . put Vaseline on our faces . . . polished our run down shoes . . . patched our dresses . . . wore sweaters so that we could wear coats . . . who welcomed us and our children . . . when we were left alone to rear them . . . who said "Get your education . . . and nobody can put you back"

This is not a poem . . . No . . . It is a celebration of the road we have traveled . . . It is a prayer . . . for the roads yet to come . . . This is an explosion . . . The original Big Bang . . . that makes the world a hopeful . . . loving place

This is the Black woman . . . in all our trouble and glory . . . in all our past history and future forbearance . . . in all that ever made love a possibility. . . . . . . . . . . . . . . . . . . . . .This is about us . . .
    bleached and natural . . . braided and straightened hair . . .
    made up . . . or . . . beaten up faces . . .
    tall . . . short . . . stately . . . bent . . .
    CC Riders . . . junkies . . . whores . . .
    wives . . . mothers . . . grandmothers . . . aunts
    working in the home or outside . . .
    working in the system or outside . . .
    working praying working to survive . . .
    giving pride . . . giving succor . . . giving voice . . . giving
    encouragement . . . giving whatever . . . we can give

This is a flag . . . that we placed over Peter Salem and Peter Poor . . . the 54th Regiment from Massachusetts . . . All the men and women lynched in the name of rape . . . Emmett Till . . . Medgar Evers . . . Malcolm X . . . Martin Luther King, Jr. . . . This a banner we fly for Respect . . . Dignity . . . the Assumption of Integrity . . . for a future generation to rally around

This is about us . . . Celebrating ourselves . . . And a well deserved honor it is . . . Light the candles, Essence . . . This is a rocket . . . Let's ride

*Black*

# Feeling

*Black* **Talk/**

*Black*

# Judgement

## Detroit Conference of Unity and Art
(For HRB)

We went there to confer
On the possibility of
Blackness
And the inevitability of
Revolution

We talked about
Black leaders
And
Black Love

We talked about
Women
And Black men

No doubt many important
Resolutions
Were passed
As we climbed Malcolm's ladder

But the most
Valid of them
All was that
Rap chose me

## On Hearing "The Girl with the Flaxen Hair"

He has a girl who has flaxen hair
My woman has hair of gray
I have a woman who wakes up at dawn
His girl can sleep through the day

His girl has hands soothed with perfumes sweet
She has lips soft and pink
My woman's lips burn in midday sun
My woman's hands—black like ink

He can make music to please his girl
Night comes I'm tired and beat
He can make notes, make her heart beat fast
Night comes I want off my feet

Maybe if I don't pick cotton so fast
Maybe I'd sing pretty too
Sing to my woman with hair of gray
Croon softly, Baby it's you

# You Came, Too

I came to the crowd seeking friends
I came to the crowd seeking love
I came to the crowd for understanding

I found you

I came to the crowd to weep
I came to the crowd to laugh

You dried my tears
You shared my happiness

I went from the crowd seeking you
I went from the crowd seeking me
I went from the crowd forever

You came, too

# Poem
*(For BMC No. 1)*

I stood still and was a mushroom on the forest green
With all the *moiles* conferring as to my edibility
It stormed and there was no leaf to cover me
I was water-logged (having absorbed all that I could)
I dreamed I was drowning
That no sun from Venice would dry my tears
But a silly green cricket with a pink umbrella said
Hello     Tell me about it
And we talked our way through the storm

Perhaps we could have found an inn
Or at least a rainbow somewhere over
But they always said
Only one     Only one more
And Christmas being so near
We over identified

Though I worship nothing (save myself)
You were my savior—so be it
And it was
Perhaps not never more or ever after
But after all—once you were mine

# Poem

*(For BMC No. 2)*

There were fields where once we walked
Among the clover and crab grass and those
Funny little things that look like cotton candy

There were liquids expanding and contracting
In which we swam with amoebas and other Afro-Americans

The sun was no further than my hand from your hair

Those were barefoot boy with cheeks of tan days
And I was John Henry hammering to get in

I was the camel with a cold nose

Now, having the tent, I have no use for it
I have pushed you out

Go 'way
Can't you see I'm lonely

## Poem
*(For PCH)*

And this silly wire
(which some consider essential)
Connected us
And we came together

So I put my arms around you to keep you
From falling from a tree
(there is evidence that you have climbed
too far up and are not at all functional
with this atmosphere or terrain)
And if I had a spare
I'd lend you my oxygen tent

But you know how selfish people are
When they have something at stake

So we sit between a line of
Daggers
And if all goes well

They will write Someday
That you and I did it

And we never even thought for sure
(if thought was one of the processes we employed)
That it could be done

# Poem
*(No Name No. 1)*

And every now and then I think
About the river

Where once we sat
Upon the bank
Which
You robbed

And I let you
Wasn't it fun

## Poem
*(For BMC No. 3)*


But I had called the office
And the voice across the line
Swore up and down (and maybe
all the way 'round)
That you wouldn't be in

Until 11:00 A.M.

So I took a chance
And dialed your phone

And was really quite content
After you said
Hello

But since I had previously
Been taught
By you especially
That you won't say
Hello
More than once

I picked a fight

## Black Separatism

It starts with a hand
Reaching out in the night
And pretended sleep

We may talk about our day
At the office
Then again
Baseball scores are just
As valid
As the comic page
At break fast

The only thing that really
Matters
Is that it comes

And we talk about the kids
Signing our letters

YOURS FOR FREEDOM

# Poem

*(No Name No. 2)*

Bitter Black Bitterness
Black Bitter Bitterness
Bitterness Black Brothers
Bitter Black Get
Blacker Get Bitter
Get Black Bitterness
NOW

# Poem
*(No Name No. 3)*

The Black Revolution is passing you bye
negroes
Anne Frank didn't put cheese and bread away for you
Because she knew it would be different this time
The naziboots don't march this year
Won't march next year
Won't come to pick you up in a
honka honka VW bus
So don't wait for that
negroes
They already got Malcolm
They already got LeRoi
They already strapped a harness on Rap
They already pulled Stokely's teeth
They already here if you can hear properly
negroes
Didn't you hear them when 40 thousand Indians died
from exposure to
honkies
Didn't you hear them when Viet children died from
exposure to napalm
Can't you hear them when Arab women die from
exposure to isrealijews
You hear them while you die from exposure to wine
and poverty programs
If you hear properly
negroes
Tomorrow was too late to properly arm yourself
See can you do an improper job now
See can you do now something, anything, but move now
negro
If the Black Revolution passes you bye it's for damned
sure
the whi-te reaction to it won't

# I'm Not Lonely

i'm not lonely
sleeping all alone

you think i'm scared
but i'm a big girl
i don't cry
or anything

i have a great
big bed
to roll around
in and lots of space
and i don't dream
bad dreams
like i used
to have that you
were leaving me
anymore

now that you're gone
i don't dream
and no matter
what you think
i'm not lonely
sleeping
all alone

## For an Intellectual Audience

i'm a happy *moile*
the opposite of which
is an unhappy
*womblie*

and the only way you'll ever
understand
this poem
is if you sit
on your ear
three times a day
facing south
justa whistling
dixie
while nikki picks
her nose

if you miss nose
picking time
then you must collect
three and one half milligrams
of toe jam
and give it to barbara's cat
and if you can't find
barbara's cat

then how you gonna call
yourself
a black man?

# Black Power
(For All the Beautiful Black Panthers East)


But the whole thing is a miracle—See?

We were just standing there
talking—not touching or smoking
Pot
When this cop told
Tyrone
Move along buddy—take your whores
outa here

And this tremendous growl
From out of nowhere
Pounced on him

Nobody to this very day
Can explain
How it happened

And none of the zoos or circuses
Within fifty miles
Had reported
A panther
Missing

# Seduction

one day
you gonna walk in this house
and i'm gonna have on a long African
gown
you'll sit down and say "The Black . . ."
and i'm gonna take one arm out
then you—not noticing me at all—will say "What about
this brother . . ."
and i'm going to be slipping it over my head
and you'll rap on about "The revolution . . ."
while i rest your hand against my stomach
you'll go on—as you always do—saying
"I just can't dig . . ."
while i'm moving your hand up and down
and i'll be taking your dashiki off
then you'll say "What we really need . . ."
and i'll be licking your arm
and "The way I see it we ought to . . ."
and unbuckling your pants
"And what about the situation . . ."
and taking your shorts off
then you'll notice
your state of undress
and knowing you you'll just say
"Nikki,
isn't this counterrevolutionary . . . ?"

# Word Poem
*(Perhaps Worth Considering)*

as things be/come
let's destroy
then we can destroy
what we be/come
let's build
what we become
when we dream

# Poem for Black Boys
## (With Special Love to James)

Where are your heroes, my little Black ones
You are the Indian you so disdainfully shoot
Not the big bad sheriff on his faggoty white horse

You should play run-away-slave
or Mau Mau
These are more in line with your history

Ask your mothers for a Rap Brown gun
Santa just may comply if you wish hard enough
Ask for CULLURD instead of Monopoly
DO NOT SIT IN DO NOT FOLLOW KING
GO DIRECTLY TO STREETS
This is a game you can win

As you sit there with your all understanding eyes
You know the truth of what I'm saying
Play Back-to-Black
Grow a natural and practice vandalism
These are useful games (some say a skill is even learned)

There is a new game I must tell you of
It's called Catch the Leader Lying
(and knowing your sense of the absurd
you will enjoy this)

Also a company called Revolution has just issued
a special kit for little boys
called Burn Baby
I'm told it has full instructions on how to siphon gas
and fill a bottle

Then our old friend Hide and Seek becomes valid
Because we have much to seek and ourselves to hide
from a lecherous dog

And this poem I give is worth much more
than any nickel bag
or ten cent toy
And you will understand all too soon
That you, my children of battle, are your heroes
You must invent your own games and teach us old ones
how to play

## The Funeral of
## Martin Luther King, Jr.

His headstone said
FREE AT LAST, FREE AT LAST
But death is a slave's freedom
We seek the freedom of free men
And the construction of a world
Where Martin Luther King could have lived
and preached non-violence

## Nikki-Rosa

childhood remembrances are always a drag
if you're Black
you always remember things like living in Woodlawn
with no inside toilet
and if you become famous or something
they never talk about how happy you were to have
your mother
all to yourself and
how good the water felt when you got your bath
from one of those
big tubs that folk in chicago barbecue in
and somehow when you talk about home
it never gets across how much you
understood their feelings
as the whole family attended meetings about Hollydale
and even though you remember
your biographers never understand
your father's pain as he sells his stock
and another dream goes
And though you're poor it isn't poverty that
concerns you
and though they fought a lot
it isn't your father's drinking that makes any difference
but only that everybody is together and you
and your sister have happy birthdays and very good
Christmases
and I really hope no white person ever has cause
to write about me
because they never understand
Black love is Black wealth and they'll
probably talk about my hard childhood
and never understand that
all the while I was quite happy

# The Great Pax Whitie

In the beginning was the word
And the word was
Death
And the word was nigger
And the word was death to all niggers
And the word was death to all life
And the word was death to all
    peace be still

The genesis was life
The genesis was death
In the genesis of death
Was the genesis of war
    be still peace be still

In the name of peace
They waged the wars
    ain't they got no shame

In the name of peace
Lot's wife is now a product of the Morton company
    nah, they ain't got no shame

Noah packing his wife and kiddies up for a holiday
row row row your boat
But why'd you leave the unicorns, noah
Huh? why'd you leave them
While our Black Madonna stood there
Eighteen feet high holding Him in her arms
Listening to the rumblings of peace
    be still be still

CAN I GET A WITNESS? WITNESS? WITNESS?
He wanted to know
And peter only asked who is that dude?
Who is that Black dude?
Looks like a troublemaker to me
And the foundations of the mighty mighty
Ro Man Cat holic church were laid

    hallelujah jesus
    nah, they ain't got no shame

Cause they killed the Carthaginians
in the great appian way
And they killed the Moors
"to civilize a nation"
And they just killed the earth
And blew out the sun
In the name of a god
Whose genesis was white
And war wooed god
And america was born
Where war became peace
And genocide patriotism
And honor is a happy slave
cause all god's chillun need rhythm
And glory hallelujah why can't peace
    be still

The great emancipator was a bigot
    ain't they got no shame
And making the world safe for democracy
Were twenty million slaves
    nah, they ain't got no shame

And they barbecued six million
To raise the price of beef
And crossed the 38th parallel
To control the price of rice
    ain't we never gonna see the light

And champagne was shipped out of the East
While kosher pork was introduced
To Africa
    Only the torch can show the way

In the beginning was the deed
And the deed was death

And the honkies are getting confused
    peace be still

So the great white prince
Was shot like a nigger in texas
And our Black shining prince was murdered
like that thug in his cathedral
While our nigger in memphis
was shot like their prince in dallas
And my lord
ain't we never gonna see the light
The rumblings of this peace must be stilled
    be stilled be still

ahh Black people
ain't we got no pride?

## Intellectualism

sometimes i feel like i just get in
everybody's way
when i was a little girl
i used to go read
or make fudge
when i got bigger i
read
or picked my nose
that's what they called
intelligence
or when i got older
intellectualism
but it was only
that i was in the way

# Universality

You see boy
is universal
It can be a
man
a woman
a child
or anything—
but normally it's
a
nigger
I was told

## Knoxville, Tennessee

I always like summer
best
you can eat fresh corn
from daddy's garden
and okra
and greens
and cabbage
and lots of
barbecue
and buttermilk
and homemade ice-cream
at the church picnic
and listen to
gospel music
outside
at the church
homecoming
and go to the mountains with
your grandmother
and go barefooted
and be warm
all the time
not only when you go to bed
and sleep

# Adulthood

### (For Claudia)

i usta wonder who i'd be
when i was a little girl in indianapolis
sitting on doctors' porches with post-dawn pre-debs
(wondering would my aunt drag me to church sunday)
i was meaningless
and i wondered if life
would give me a chance to mean

i found a new life in the withdrawal from all things
not like my image

when i was a teen-ager i usta sit
on front steps conversing
the gym teacher's son with embryonic eyes
about the essential essence of the universe
(and other bullshit stuff)
recognizing the basic powerlessness of me

but then i went to college where i learned
that just because everything i was was unreal
i could be real and not just real through withdrawal
into emotional crosshairs or colored bourgeois
intellectual pretensions
but from involvement with things approaching reality
i could possibly have a life

so catatonic emotions and time wasting sex games
were replaced with functioning commitments to logic
and
necessity and the gray area was slowly darkened into
a Black thing

for a while progress was being made along with a certain degree
of happiness cause i wrote a book and found a love
and organized a theatre and even gave some lectures on
Black history
and began to believe all good people could get
together and win without bloodshed
then
hammeraskjöld was killed
and lumumba was killed
and diem was killed
and kennedy was killed
and malcolm was killed
and evers was killed
and schwerner, chaney and goodman were killed
and liuzzo was killed
and stokely fled the country
and leroi was arrested
and rap was arrested
and pollard, thompson and cooper were killed
and king was killed
and kennedy was killed
and i sometimes wonder why i didn't become a
debutante
sitting on porches, going to church all the time,
wondering
is my eye make-up on straight
or a withdrawn discoursing on the stars and moon
instead of a for real Black person who must now feel
and inflict
pain

# Dreams

in my younger years
before i learned
black people aren't
suppose to dream
i wanted to be
a raelet
and say "dr o wn d in my youn tears"
or "tal kin bout tal kin bout"
or marjorie hendricks and grind
all up against the mic
and scream
"baaaaaby nightandday
baaaaaby nightandday"
then as i grew and matured
i became more sensible
and decided i would
settle down
and just become
a sweet inspiration

# Revolutionary Music

you've just got to dig sly
and the family stone
damn the words
you gonna be dancing to the music
james brown can go to
viet nam
or sing about whatever he
has to
since he already told
the honkie
"although you happy you better try
to get along
money won't change you
but time is taking you on"
not to mention
doing a whole
song they can't even snap
their fingers to
"good god! ugh!"
talking bout
"i got the feeling baby i got the feeling"
and "hey everybody let me tell you the news"
martha and the vandellas dancing in the streets
while shorty long is functioning at that junction
yeah we hip to that

aretha said they better
think
but she already said
"ain't no way to love you"
(and you know she wasn't talking to us)
and dig the o'jays asking "must i always be a stand in
for love"
i mean they say "i'm a fool for being myself"

While the mighty mighty impressions have told the
world
for once and for all
"We're a Winner"
even our names—le roi has said—are together
impressions
temptations
supremes
delfonics
miracles
intruders (i mean intruders?)
not beatles and animals and white bad things like
young rascals and shit
we be digging all
our revolutionary music consciously or un
cause sam cooke said "a change is gonna come"

## Beautiful Black Men
**(With compliments and apologies
to all not mentioned by name)**

i wanta say just gotta say something
bout those beautiful beautiful beautiful outasight
black men
with they afros
walking down the street
is the same ol danger
but a brand new pleasure

sitting on stoops, in bars, going to offices
running numbers, watching for their whores
preaching in churches, driving their hogs
walking their dogs, winking at me
in their fire red, lime green, burnt orange
royal blue tight tight pants that hug
what i like to hug

jerry butler, wilson pickett, the impressions
temptations, mighty mighty sly
don't have to do anything but walk
on stage
and i scream and stamp and shout
see new breed men in breed alls
dashiki suits with shirts that match
the lining that complements the ties
that smile at the sandals
where dirty toes peek at me
and i scream and stamp and shout
for more beautiful beautiful beautiful
black men with outasight afros

# Woman Poem

you see, my whole life
is tied up
to unhappiness
it's father cooking breakfast
and me getting fat as a hog
or having no food
at all and father proving
his incompetence
again
i wish i knew how it would feel
to be free

it's having a job
they won't let you work
or no work at all
castrating me
(yes it happens to women too)

it's a sex object if you're pretty
and no love
or love and no sex if you're fat
get back fat black woman be a mother
grandmother strong thing but not woman
gameswoman romantic woman love needer
man seeker dick eater sweat getter
fuck needing love seeking woman

it's a hole in your shoe
and buying lil' sis a dress
and her saying you shouldn't
when you know
all too well–that you shouldn't

but smiles are only something we give
to properly dressed social workers
not each other
only smiles of i know
your game sister
which isn't really
a smile

joy is finding a pregnant roach
and squashing it
not finding someone to hold
let go get off get back don't turn
me on you black dog
how dare you care
about me
you ain't got no good sense
cause i ain't shit you must be lower
than that to care

it's a filthy house
with yesterday's watermelon
and monday's tears
cause true ladies don't
know how to clean

it's intellectual devastation
of everybody
to avoid emotional commitment
"yeah honey i would've married
him but he didn't have no degree"

it's knock-kneed mini-skirted
wig wearing died blond mama's scar
born dead my scorn your whore
rough heeled broken nailed powdered
face me
whose whole life is tied
up to unhappiness
cause it's the only
for real thing
i
know

# For Saundra

i wanted to write
a poem
that rhymes
but revolution doesn't lend
itself to be-bopping

then my neighbor
who thinks i hate
asked—do you ever write
tree poems—i like trees
so i thought
i'll write a beautiful green tree poem
peeked from my window
to check the image
noticed the school yard was covered
with asphalt
no green—no trees grow
in manhattan

then, well, i thought the sky
i'll do a big blue sky poem
but all the clouds have winged
low since no-Dick was elected

so i thought again
and it occurred to me

maybe i shouldn't write
at all
but clean my gun
and check my kerosene supply

perhaps these are not poetic
times
at all

# Balances

in life
one is always
balancing

like we juggle our mothers
against our fathers

or one teacher
against another
(only to balance our grade average)

3 grains salt
to one ounce truth

our sweet black essence
or the funky honkies down the street

and lately i've begun wondering
if you're trying to tell me something

we used to talk all night
and do things alone together

and i've begun
(as a reaction to a feeling)
to balance
the pleasure of loneliness
against the pain
of loving you

# For Theresa

and when i was all alone
facing my adolescence
looking forward
to cleaning house
and reading books
and maybe learning bridge
so that i could fit
into acceptable society
acceptably
you came along
and loved me
for being black and bitchy
hateful and scared
and you came along
and cared that i got
all the things necessary
to adulthood
and even made sure
i wouldn't hate
my mother
or father
and you even understood
that i should love
peppe
but not too much
and give to gary
but not all of me
and keep on moving
'til i found me
and now you're sick
and have been hurt
for some time
and i've felt guilty
and impotent
for not being able

to give yourself
to you
as you gave
yourself
to me

# My Poem

i am 25 years old
black female poet
wrote a poem asking
nigger can you kill
if they kill me
it won't stop
the revolution

i have been robbed
it looked like they knew
that i was to be hit
they took my tv
my two rings
my piece of african print
and my two guns
if they take my life
it won't stop
the revolution

my phone is tapped
my mail is opened
they've caused me to turn
on all my old friends
and all my new lovers
if i hate all black
people
and all negroes
it won't stop
the revolution

i'm afraid to tell
my roommate where i'm going
and scared to tell
people if i'm coming
if i sit here
for the rest
of my life
it won't stop
the revolution

if i never write
another poem
or short story
if i flunk out
of grad school
if my car is reclaimed
and my record player
won't play
and if i never see
a peaceful day
or do a meaningful
black thing
it won't stop
the revolution
the revolution
is in the streets
and if i stay on
the 5th floor

it will go on
if i never do
anything
it will go on

## For Tommy

to tommy who:
eats chocolate cookies and lamb chops
climbs stairs and cries when i change
    his diaper
lets me hold him only on his schedule
defined my nature
and gave me a new name (mommy)
which supersedes all others
controls my life
and makes me glad
that he does

## No Reservations
(For Art Jones)

there are no reservations
for the revolution

no polite little clerk
to send notice
to your room
saying you are WANTED
on the battlefield

there are no banners
to wave you forward
no blaring trumpets
not even a blues note
moaning wailing lone blue note
to the yoruba drums saying
strike now     shoot
strike now     fire
strike now     run

there will be no grand
parade
and a lot thrown round
your neck
people won't look up and say
"why he used to live next to me
isn't it nice
it's his turn now"

there will be no recruitment
station
where you can give
the most convenient hours
"monday wednesday i play ball
friday night i play cards
any other time i'm free"

there will be no reserve
of energy
no slacking off till next time
"let's see—i can come back
next week
better not wear myself out
this time"

there will be reservations
only
if we fail

## Alone

i can be
alone by myself
i was
lonely alone
now i'm lonely
with you
something is wrong
there are flies
everywhere
i go

## For Two Jameses
(Ballantine and Snow)
In iron cells

we all start
as a speck
nobody notices us
but some may hope
we're there
some count days and wait

we grow
in a cell that spreads
like a summer cold
to other people
they notice and laugh
some are happy
some wish to stop
our movement

we kick and move
are stubborn and demanding
completely inside
the system

they put us in a cell
to make us behave
never realizing it's from cells
we have escaped
and we will be born
from their iron cells
new people with a new cry

## Autumn Poems

the heat
you left with me
last night
still smolders
the wind catches
your scent
and refreshes
my senses


i am a leaf
falling from your tree
upon which i was
impaled

# Rain

rain is
god's sperm falling
in the receptive
woman how else
to spend
a rainy day
other than with you
seeking sun and stars
and heavenly bodies
how else to spend
a rainy day
other than with you

## Housecleaning

i always liked house cleaning
even as a child
i dug straightening
the cabinets
putting new paper on
the shelves
washing the refrigerator
inside out
and unfortunately this habit has
carried over and i find
i must remove you
from my life

# Poem For Aretha

cause nobody deals with aretha—a mother with four
    children—having to hit the road
they always say "after she comes
home" but nobody ever says what it's like
to get on a plane for a three week tour
the elation of the first couple of audiences the good
feeling of exchange the running on the high
you get from singing good
and loud and long telling the world
what's on your mind

then comes the eighth show on the sixth day the beginning
to smell like the plane or bus the if-you-forget-your-tooth-
    brush
in-one-spot-you-can't-brush-until-the-second-show the
    strangers
pulling at you cause they love you but you having no love
to give back
the singing the same songs night after night day after day
and if you read the gossip columns the rumors that your
    husband
is only after your fame
the wondering if your children will be glad to see you and
    maybe
the not caring if they are the scheming to get out
of just one show and go just one place where some doe-
    doe-dupaduke
won't say "just sing one song, please"

nobody mentions how it feels to become a freak
because you have talent and how
no one gives a damn how you feel
but only cares that aretha franklin is here like maybe that'll
stop:

chickens from frying
eggs from being laid
crackers from hating


and if you say you're lonely or scared or tired how they
     always
just say "oh come off it" or "did you see
how they loved you did you see huh did you?"
which most likely has nothing to do with you anyway
and i'm not saying aretha shouldn't have talent and i'm
     certainly
not saying she should quit
singing but as much as i love her i'd vote "yes" to her
doing four concerts a year and staying home or doing what-
     ever
she wants and making records cause it's a shame
the way we are killing her
we eat up artists like there's going to be a famine at the
     end
of those three minutes when there are in fact an abundance
of talents just waiting let's put some
of the giants away for a while and deal with them like they
     have
a life to lead


aretha doesn't have to relive billie holiday's life doesn't
     have
to relive dinah washington's death but who will
stop the pattern

she's more important than her music—if they must be
      separated—
and they should be separated when she has to pass out
      before
anyone recognizes she needs
a rest and i say i need
aretha's music
she is undoubtedly the one person who put everyone on
notice
she revived johnny ace and remembered lil green aretha
      sings
"i say a little prayer" and dionne doesn't
want to hear it anymore
aretha sings "money won't change you"
but james can't sing "respect" the advent
of aretha pulled ray charles from marlboro country
and back into
the blues made nancy wilson
try one more time forced
dionne to make a choice (she opted for the movies)
and diana ross had to get an afro wig pushed every
Black singer into Blackness and negro entertainers
into negroness you couldn't jive
when she said "you make me/feel" the blazers
had to reply "gotta let a man be/a man"
aretha said "when my soul was in the lost and found/you
      came
along to claim it" and joplin said "maybe"
there has been no musician whom her very presence hasn't
affected when humphrey wanted her to campaign she said
"woeman's only hueman"
and he pressured james brown
they removed otis cause the combination was too strong
the impressions had to say "lord have mercy/we're moving
on up"

the Black songs started coming from the singers on stage
        and the dancers
in the streets
aretha was the riot was the leader if she had said "come
let's do it" it would have been done
temptations say why don't we think about it
                                think about it
                                think about it

# Revolutionary Dreams

i used to dream militant
dreams of taking
over america to show
these white folks how it should be
done
i used to dream radical dreams
of blowing everyone away with my perceptive powers
of correct analysis
i even used to think i'd be the one
to stop the riot and negotiate the peace
then i awoke and dug
that if i dreamed natural
dreams of being a natural
woman doing what a woman
does when she's natural
i would have a revolution

## Walking Down Park

walking down park
amsterdam
or columbus do you ever stop
to think what it looked like
before it was an avenue
did you ever stop to think
what you walked
before you rode
subways to the stock
exchange (we can't be on
the stock exchange
we are the stock
exchanged)

did you ever maybe wonder
what grass was like before
they rolled it
into a ball and called
it central park
where syphilitic dogs
and their two-legged tubercular
masters fertilize
the corners and side-walks
ever want to know what would happen
if your life could be fertilized
by a love thought
from a loved one
who loves you

ever look south
on a clear day and not see
time's squares but see
tall Birch trees with sycamores
touching hands
and see gazelles running playfully
after the lions
ever hear the antelope bark
from the third floor apartment

ever, did you ever, sit down
and wonder about what freedom's freedom
would bring
it's so easy to be free
you start by loving yourself
then those who look like you
all else will come
naturally

ever wonder why
so much asphalt was laid
in so little space
probably so we would forget
the Iroquois, Algonquin
and Mohicans who could caress
the earth

ever think what Harlem would be
like if our herbs and roots and elephant ears
grew sending
a cacophony of sound to us
the parrot parroting black is beautiful black is beautiful
owls sending out whooooo's making love . . .
and me and you just sitting in the sun trying
to find a way to get a banana from one of the monkeys
koala bears in the trees laughing at our listlessness

ever think it's possible
for us to be
happy

## Kidnap Poem

ever been kidnapped
by a poet
if i were a poet
i'd kidnap you
put you in my phrases and meter
you to jones beach
or maybe coney island
or maybe just to my house
lyric you in lilacs
dash you in the rain
blend into the beach
to complement my see
play the lyre for you
ode you with my love song
anything to win you
wrap you in the red Black green
show you off to mama
yeah if i were a poet i'd kid
nap you

# The Geni In The Jar

(For Nina Simone)

take a note and spin it around spin it around don't
prick your finger
take a note and spin it around
on the Black loom on the Black loom
careful baby
don't prick your finger

take the air and weave the sky
around the Black loom around the Black loom
make the sky sing a Black song sing a blue song
sing my song make the sky sing a Black song
from the Black loom from the Black loom
careful baby
don't prick your finger

take the geni and put her in a jar
put her in a jar
wrap the sky around her
take the geni and put her in a jar
wrap the sky around her
listen to her sing
sing a Black song our Black song
from the Black loom
singing to me
from the Black loom
careful baby
don't prick your finger

## All I Gotta Do

all i gotta do
is sit and wait
sit and wait
and it's gonna find
me
all i gotta do
is sit and wait
if i can learn
how

what i need to do
is sit and wait
cause i'm a woman
sit and wait
what i gotta do
is sit and wait
cause i'm a woman
it'll find me

you get yours
and i'll get mine
if i learn
to sit and wait
you got yours
i want mine
and i'm gonna get it
cause i gotta get it
cause i need to get it
if i learn how

thought about calling
for it on the phone
asked for a delivery
but they didn't have it
thought about going
to the store to get it
walked to the corner
but they didn't have it

called your name
in my sleep
sitting and waiting
thought you would awake me
called your name
lying in my bed
but you didn't have it
offered to go get it
but you didn't have it
so i'm sitting

all i know
is sitting and waiting
waiting and sitting
cause i'm a woman
all i know
is sitting and waiting
cause i gotta wait
wait for it to find
me

# Master Charge Blues

it's wednesday night baby
and i'm all alone
wednesday night baby
and i'm all alone
sitting with myself
waiting for the telephone

wanted you baby
but you said you had to go
wanted you yeah
but you said you had to go
called your best friend
but he can't come 'cross no more

did you ever go to bed
at the end of a busy day
look over and see the smooth
where your hump usta lay
feminine odor and no reason why
i said feminine odor and no reason why
asked the lord to help me
he shook his head "not i"

but i'm a modern woman baby
ain't gonna let this get me down
i'm a modern woman
ain't gonna let this get me down
gonna take my master charge
and get everything in town

# For A Lady Of Pleasure Now Retired

some small island birthed
her and a big (probably) white ship took her
from mother to come
to america's recreation

she lives in the top of my building
i only know her through her eyes
she is old now not only from years
but from aging

one gets the impression she was most
beautiful and like good wine
or a semiprecious jewel touted out
for the pleasure of those
who could afford
her recreation

her head is always high
though the set of her mouth shows
it's not easy
she asks nothing
seems to have something
to give but no one to give it
to if ever she gave it
to anyone

age requires happy memories like louvenia smiled
when she died and though her doctor had told her not
to there was pork cooking
on the stove
there are so many new mistakes
for a lady of pleasure
that can be made it shouldn't be
necessary to repeat the old
ones

and it was cold
on the elevator that morning
when i spoke to her and foolishly asked
    how are you
she smiled and tilted her head
    at least, i said, the sun is
    shining
and her eyes smiled      yes
and i was glad to be
there to say through spirits
    there is a new creation
to her

## Alabama Poem

if trees could talk
 wonder what they'd say
met an old man
 on the road late after noon
 hat pulled over to shade
 his eyes
 jacket slumped over his
 shoulders
 told me "girl! my hands seen
 more than all
 them books they got
 at tuskegee"
 smiled at me
 half waved his hand
 walked on down the dusty road
met an old woman
 with a corncob pipe
 sitting and rocking
 on a spring evening
 "sista" she called to me
 "let me tell you—my feet
 seen more than yo eyes
 ever gonna read"
 smiled at her and kept
 on moving
 gave it a thought and went
 back to the porch
 "i say gal" she called down
 "you a student at the institute?
 better come here and study
 these feet

i'm gonna cut a bunion off
soon's i gets up"
i looked at her
she laughed at me
if trees would talk
wonder what they'd tell me

# Ego Tripping

*(there may be a reason why)*

I was born in the congo
I walked to the fertile crescent and built
    the sphinx
I designed a pyramid so tough that a star
      that only glows every one hundred years falls
      into the center giving divine perfect light
I am bad

I sat on the throne
    drinking nectar with allah
I got hot and sent an ice age to europe
    to cool my thirst
My oldest daughter is nefertiti
    the tears from my birth pains
    created the nile
I am a beautiful woman

I gazed on the forest and burned
    out the sahara desert
    with a packet of goat's meat
and a change of clothes
I crossed it in two hours
I am a gazelle so swift
    so swift you can't catch me

    For a birthday present when he was three
I gave my son hannibal an elephant
    He gave me rome for mother's day
My strength flows ever on

My son noah built new/ark and
I stood proudly at the helm
    as we sailed on a soft summer day
I turned myself into myself and was
    jesus
    men intone my loving name
    All praises All praises
I am the one who would save

I sowed diamonds in my back yard
My bowels deliver uranium
    the filings from my fingernails are
    semi-precious jewels
    On a trip north
I caught a cold and blew
My nose giving oil to the arab world
I am so hip even my errors are correct
I sailed west to reach east and had to round off
    the earth as I went
    The hair from my head thinned and gold was laid
    across three continents

I am so perfect so divine so ethereal so surreal
I cannot be comprehended
    except by my permission

I mean . . . I . . . can fly
    like a bird in the sky . . .

## Poem For Flora

when she was little
and colored and ugly with short
straightened hair
and a very pretty smile
she went to sunday school to hear
'bout nebuchadnezzar the king
of the jews

and she would listen

shadrach, meshach and abednego in the fire

and she would learn

how god was neither north
nor south east or west
with no color but all
she remembered was that
Sheba was Black and comely

and she would think

i want to be
like that

## Sometimes

sometimes
when i wake up
in the morning
and see all the faces
i just can't
breathe

# Poem For A Lady Whose Voice I Like

so he said: you ain't got no talent
    if you didn't have a face
    you wouldn't be nobody

and she said: god created heaven and earth
    and all that's Black within them

so he said: you ain't really no hot shit
    they tell me plenty sisters
    take care better business than you

and she said: on the third day he made chitterlings
    and all good things to eat
    and said: "that's good"

so he said: if the white folks hadn't been under
    yo skirt and been giving you the big play
    you'd a had to come on uptown like everybody else

and she replied: then he took a big Black greasy rib
    from adam and said we will call this woeman and her
    name will be sapphire and she will divide into four
    parts
    that simone may sing a song

and he said: you pretty full of yourself ain't chu

so she replied: show me someone not full of herself
    and i'll show you an empty person

# How Do You Write A Poem?

how do you write a poem
about someone so close
to you that when you say ahhhhh
they say chuuuu
what can they ask you to put
on paper that isn't already written
on your face
and does the paper make it
any more real
that without them
life would be not
impossible but certainly
more difficult
and why would someone need
a poem to say when i come
home if you're not there
i search the air
for your scent
would i search any less
if i told the world
i don't care at all
and love is so complete
that touch or not we blend
to each other the things
that matter aren't all about
baaaanging (i can be baaaanged all
day long) but finding a spot
where i can be free
of all the physical
and emotional bullshit
and simply sit with a cup
of coffee and say to you
"i'm tired" don't you know
those are my love words

and say to you "how was your
day" doesn't that show
i care or say to you "we lost
a friend" and not want to share
that loss with strangers
don't you already know
what i feel and if
you don't maybe
i should check my feelings

# And Sometimes I Sit

and sometimes i sit
down at my typewriter
and i think
not of someone
cause there isn't anyone
to think
about and i wonder
is it worth it

# I Want To Sing

i want to sing
a piercing note
lazily throwing my legs
across the moon
my voice carrying all the way
over to your pillow
    i want you

i need i swear to loll
about the sun
and have it smelt me
the ionosphere carrying
my ashes all
the way over
to your pillow
    i want you

## Ever Want To Crawl

ever want to crawl
in someone's arms
white out the world
in someone's arms
and feel the world
of someone's arms
it's so hot in hell
if i don't sweat
i'll melt

# Broadside:

*Poem of*

## Angela *Yvonne*

# Davis

# Poem of Angela Yvonne Davis

*(October 16, 1970)*

i move on feeling and have learned to distrust those who
    don't
i move in time and space determined by time and space
    feeling
that all is natural and i am
a part of it and "how could you?" they ask you had
    everything
but the men who killed the children in birmingham aren't
    on
the most wanted list and the men who killed schwerner,
    chaney
and goodman aren't on the most wanted list and the list of
    names
unlisted could and probably would include most of our
    "finest
leaders" who are WANTED in my estimation for at least
    serious
questioning so we made a list and listed it

"but you had everything." they said and i asked
    "quakers?" and i asked
"jews?" and i asked "being sent from home?" my mother
    told me the world
would one day speak my name then she recently suggested
    angela yvonne
why don't you take up sports like your brother and i said "i
    don't run
as well as he" but they told me over and over again "you
    can have them
all at your feet" though i knew they were at my feet when
    i was born
and the heavens opened up sending the same streak of
    lightening through
my mother as through new york when i was arrested

and i saw my sisters and brothers and i heard them tell the
young
racists "you can't march with us" and i thought i can't
march at all
and i looked at the woman whose face was kissed by night
as she said
"angela you shall be free" and i thought i won't be free
even if i'm set
loose. the game is set the tragedy written my part is
captive
i thought of betty shabazz and the voices who must have
said "aren't you
sort of glad it's over?" with that stupidity that fails to
notice
it will never be over for some of us and our children and
our
grandchildren. betty can no more forget that staccato than i
the pain
in johnathan's face or the love in george's letters. and i
remember
the letter where i asked "why don't you write beverly
axelrod and become
rich and famous" and his complete reply

*　　*　　*

i remember water and sky and paris and wanting someone
to be mine
a german? but the world is in love with germans so why
not? though
i being the youngest daughter of africa and the sun was
rejected
and all the while them saying "isn't she beautiful?" and
she being i
thinking "aren't you sick" and i remember wanting to give
myself but
nothing being big enough to take me and searching for the
right way
to live and seeing the answer understanding the right way
to die
though death is as distasteful as the second cigarette in the
morning
and don't you understand? i value my life so surely all
others must value
theirs and that's the weakness the weak use against us.
they so
casually make decisions like who's going to live and who's
going to
starve to death and who will be happy or not and they
never know
what their life means since theirs lacks meaning and they
never
have to try to understand what some else's life could mean
those guards and policemen who so casually take the only
possession
worth possessing and dispense with it like an empty r.c.
cola bottle
never understanding the vitality of its contents

and the white boys and girls came with their little erections
and i
learned to see but not show feeling and i learned to talk
while not
screaming though i would scream if anyone understands
that language
and i would reach if there were a substance and Black
people say
i went communist and i only and always thought i went
and Black people
say "why howard johnson's" but i could think of no other
place and Black
people ask "why didn't i shoot it out?" when i thought i
had. and they say
they have no responsibility and i knew they would not rest
until my
body was brought out in tiny flabby pieces

the list is long and our basic christianity teaches us to
sacrifice
the good to the evil and if the blood is type O positive
maybe they
will be satisfied but white people are like any other gods
with an insatiatable
appetite and as long as we sacrifice our delicate to their
course we will sacrifice
i mean i started with a clear head cause i felt i should and
feeling
is much more than mere emotion though that is not to be
sacrificed
and through it all i was looking for this woman angela
yvonne

and i wanted to be harriet tubman who was the first
    WANTED Black woman
and i wanted to bring myself and us out of the fear and
    into the Dark
but my helpers trapped me and this i have learned of
    love—it is harder
to be loved than to love and the responsibilities of letting
    yourself
be loved are too great and perhaps i shall never love again
cause i would rather need than allow, and what i'm saying
    is
i had five hours of freedom when i recognized my lovers
    had decided
and i was free in my mind to say—whatever you do you
    will not know
what you have done

we walked that october afternoon among the lights and
    smells of autumn
people and i tried so to hold on. and as i turned 51st street
    and eighth
and saw, i knew there was nothing more to say so i thought
and i entered the elevator touching the insides as a woman
    is touched
i looked into the carpet as we were expelled
and entered the key
which would both open and close me
and i thought to them all
to myself just make it easy
on yourself

# *My*
# House

## Legacies

her grandmother called her from the playground
    "yes, ma'am" said the little girl
    "i want chu to learn how to make rolls" said the old
woman proudly
but the little girl didn't want
to learn how because she knew
even if she couldn't say it that
that would mean when the old one died she would be less
dependent on her spirit so
the little girl said
    "i don't want to know how to make no rolls"
with her lips poked out
and the old woman wiped her hands on
her apron saying "lord
    these children"
and neither of them ever
said what they meant
and i guess nobody ever does

# Mothers

the last time i was home
to see my mother we kissed
exchanged pleasantries
and unpleasantries pulled a warm
comforting silence around
us and read separate books

i remember the first time
i consciously saw her
we were living in a three room
apartment on burns avenue

mommy always sat in the dark
i don't know how i knew that but she did

that night i stumbled into the kitchen
maybe because i've always been
a night person or perhaps because i had wet
the bed
she was sitting on a chair
the room was bathed in moonlight diffused through
    tiny window panes
she may have been smoking but maybe not
her hair was three-quarters her height
which made me a strong believer in the samson myth
and very black

i'm sure i just hung there by the door
i remember thinking: what a beautiful lady

she was very deliberately waiting
perhaps for my father to come home
from his night job or maybe for a dream
that had promised to come by
"come here" she said "i'll teach you
a poem: *i see the moon*

> *the moon sees me*
> *god bless the moon*
> *and god bless me*"

i taught that to my son
who recited it for her
just to say we must learn
to bear the pleasures
as we have borne the pains

## Winter Poem

once a snowflake fell
on my brow and i loved
it so much and i kissed
it and it was happy and called its cousins
and brothers and a web
of snow engulfed me then
i reached to love them all
and i squeezed them and they became
a spring rain and i stood perfectly
still and was a flower

# Conversation

"yeah" she said "my man's gone too
been dead longer than you is old"
"what do you do" i asked
"sit here on the porch and talk to the old folk
i rock and talk and go to church most times"
"but aren't you lonely sometimes" i asked
"now you gotta answer yo own question"
"i guess the children help a lot     you got grandchildren
haven't you"
"oh the children they come and go always in a hurry
got something to do ain't no time for old folks
like me"
she squinted at the sun packing her jaw
with *bruton* snuff
"the old days done gone . . . and i say good-bye
peoples be going to the moon and all . . . ain't that
wonderful . . . to the moon"
and i said "i see stars all the time aretha franklin
and sly were at madison square garden recently"
"what you doing here" she asked
"i'm a poet" i said
"that ain't no reason to be uppity"
and the sun beat down on my head while
a dragonfly admonished my flippancy
but a blue and yellow butterfly sat on my knee
i looked her square in the eye
"i ain't gonna tell you" she said and turned her head
"ain't gonna tell me what" i asked
"what you asking me you gotta live to be seventy-nine
fore you could understand anyhow"
"now you being uppity" i said
"yeah but i earned it" she replied and shifting her wad
she clapped her hands and smiled
"you been here before"

and i said "yes ma'am but would you tell me just one
    thing
what did i learn"
and she spat out her juice
"honey if you don't know how can i"
i wanted to argue but the sun was too hot and the sky
too lazy and god heaved a sigh
she crossed her legs at the ankle
and straightened her back
"tell you this" she said
"keep yo dress up and yo pants down and you'll be all
    right"
and i said impatiently "old lady you got it all wrong"
"honey, ain't never been wrong yet
you better get back to the city cause you one of them
technical niggers and you'll have problems here"

## Rituals

i always wanted to be a bridesmaid
honest to god
i could just see me floating
down that holy aisle leading
some dear friend to heaven
in pink and purple organza with lots and lots
of crinoline pushing the violets out from my dress
hem
or maybe in a more sophisticated endeavor
one of those lovely sky blue slinky numbers
fitting tight around my abounding twenty-eights
holding a single red rose white gloves open in the back
always forever made of nylon and my feet nestled gently
in *chandlers* number 699 which was also the price plus
one dollar to match it pretty near the dress color

wedding rituals have always intrigued me
and i'd swear to friends i wouldn't say goddamn not even
once no matter what neither would i give a power
sign but would even comb my hair severely
back and put that blue shit under my eyes
i swear i wanted to be in a wedding

# The World Is Not A Pleasant Place To Be

the world is not a pleasant place
to be without
someone to hold and be held by

a river would stop
its flow if only
a stream were there
to receive it

an ocean would never laugh
if clouds weren't there
to kiss her tears

the world is not
a pleasant place to be without
someone

# The Butterfly

those things
which you so laughingly call
hands are in fact two
brown butterflies fluttering
across the pleasure
they give
my body

# I Remember

i remember learning you jump
in your sleep and smile
when you wake up

at first you cuddle
then one arm across my stomach
then one leg touching my leg then
you turn your back

but you smile when you wake up

i was surprised to know you don't care
if your amp burns all night and that you could
play *ohmeohmy* over and over again just
because you remembered

i discovered you don't like hair
in your bathroom sink and never step
your wet feet onto a clean rug

you will answer your phone
but you don't talk too long and you do
rub my toes and make faces
while you talk
and your voice told her anyway
that i was there

you can get up at three and make sandwiches
and orange juice and tell jokes
you sometimes make incoherent sentences
you snore
and you smile when you wake up

i know you cry when you're hurt
and curse when you're angry
and try when you don't feel
like it and smile at me
when you wake up

these things i learned through
a simple single touch
when fleshes clashed

## A Certain Peace

it was very pleasant
not having you around
this afternoon

not that i don't love you
and want you and need you
and love loving and wanting and needing you

but there was a certain peace
when you walked out the door
and i knew you would do something
you wanted to do
and i could run
a tub full of water
and not worry about answering the phone
for your call
and soak in bubbles
and not worry whether you would want something
special for dinner
and rub lotion all over me
for as long as i wanted
and not worry if you had a good idea
or wanted to use the bathroom

and there was a certain excitement
when after midnight you came home
and we had coffee
and i had a day of mine
that made me as happy
as yours did you

## When I Nap

when i nap
usually after 1:30
because the sun comes
in my room then
hitting the northeast
corner

i lay at the foot
of my bed and smell
the sweat of your feet
in my covers
while i dream

## Just a New York Poem

i wanted to take
your hand and run with you
together toward
ourselves down the street to your street
i wanted to laugh aloud
and skip the notes past
the marquee advertising "women
in love" past the record
shop with "The Spirit
In The Dark" past the smoke shop
past the park and no
parking today signs
past the people watching me in
my blue velvet and i don't remember
what you wore but only that i didn't want
anything to be wearing you
i wanted to give
myself to the cyclone that is
your arms
and let you in the eye of my hurricane and know
the calm before

and some fall evening
after the cocktails
and the very expensive and very bad
steak served with day-old baked potatoes

after the second cup of coffee taken
while listening to the rejected
violin player
maybe some fall evening
when the taxis have passed you by
and that light sort of rain
that occasionally falls
in new york begins
you'll take a thought
and laugh aloud
the notes carrying all the way over
to me and we'll run again
together
toward each other
yes?

# [Untitled]

there is a hunger
    often associated with pain
    that you feel
    when you look at someone
    you used to love and enjoyed
    loving and want
    to love again
    though you know you can't
that gnaws at you
    as steadily as a mosquito
    some michigan summer
    churning his wings
    through your window screen
because the real world

| | |
|---|---|
| *made up of baby clothes* | *to be washed* |
| *food* | *to be cooked* |
| *lullabies* | *to be sung* |
| *smiles* | *to be glowed* |
| *hair* | *to be plaited* |
| *ribbons* | *to be bowed* |
| *coffee* | *to be drunk* |
| *books* | *to be read* |
| *tears* | *to be cried* |
| *loneliness* | *to be borne* |

says you are a strong woman
    and anyway he never thought you'd really miss him

# The Wonder Woman
*(A New Dream—for Stevie Wonder)*

dreams have a way
of tossing and turning themselves
around and the times
make requirements that we dream
real dreams for example
i wanted to be
a sweet inspiration in my dreams
of my people but the times
require that i give
myself willingly and become
a wonder woman

# Categories

sometimes you hear a question like "what is
your responsibility as an unwed mother"
and some other times you stand sweating profusely before
going on stage and somebody says "but you are used
    to it"
or maybe you look into a face you've never seen
or never noticed and you know
the ugly awful loneliness of being
locked into a mind and body that belong
to a *name* or *non-name*—not that it matters
cause *you* feel and *it* felt but you have
a planetrainbussubway—it doesn't matter—something
to catch to take your arms away from someone
you might have thought about
putting them around if you didn't
have all that shit to take you safely away

and sometimes on rainy nights you see
an old white woman who maybe you'd really care about
except that you're a young Black woman
whose job it is to kill maim or seriously
make her question
the validity of her existence

and you look at her kind of funny colored eyes
and you think
if she weren't such an aggressive bitch she would see
that if you weren't such a Black one
there would be a relationship but anyway—it doesn't
    matter
much—except you started out to kill her and now find
you just don't give a damn cause it's all somewhat
    of a bore
so you speak of your mother or sister or very good friend
and really you speak of your feelings which are too
    personal
for anyone else
to take a chance on feeling
and you eat that godawful food and you get somehow
through it and if this seems
like somewhat of a tentative poem it's probably
because i just realized that
i'm bored with categories

# Scrapbooks

it's funny that smells and sounds return
so all alone uncalled unneeded
on a sweaty night as i sit armed
with coffee and cigarettes waiting

sometimes it seems
my life is a scrapbook

i usta get 1.50 per week
for various duties unperformed
while i read *green dolphin street*
and *the sun is my undoing*
never understanding my exclusion
but knowing quite clearly the hero
is always misunderstood
though always right in the end

roy gave me a yellow carnation
that year for the junior prom

the red rose was from michael
who was the prettiest boy i'd ever known
he took me to the *jack and jill* dance
and left me sitting in the corner until
the slow drags came on then he danced
real tight and sweated out my bangs
i had a white leather monstrosity that passed
for taste in my adolescence pressed with dances
undanced though the songs were melodious

and somehow three or four books were filled
with proms and parties and programs that
my grandmother made me go to
for "culture" so that i could be
a lady
my favorite is the fisk book with clippings
of the *forum* and notes from the dean of women
saying "you are on social probation" and "you are
suspended from fisk"
and letters from my mother saying "behave yourself"
and letters from my grandmother reminding me
"your grandfather graduated fisk in 1905" and not
to try to run the school
but mostly notes from alvin asking when
was i coming over
again
i purchased a blue canvas notebook for the refrain

it's really something when you sit
watching dawn peep over apartment buildings
that seemed so ominous during the night and see
pages of smiling pictures      groups of girls throwing
pillows      couples staring nervously ahead as if they
think the kodak will eat them      someone with a ponytail
and a miles davis record      a lady with an afro pointing
joyously to a diploma      a girl in a brown tan and red
bathing suit holding a baby that looks like you

and now there is a black leather book filled
efficiently by a clipping service
and a pile of unanswered letters that remind
you to love those who love you
and i sit at dawn
all my defenses gone sometimes
listening to *something cool* sometimes
hearing *tears on my pillow*
and know there must be other books
filled with failures and family and friends
that perhaps one day i can unfold
for my grandchildren

## When I Die

when i die i hope no one who ever hurt me cries
and if they cry i hope their eyes fall out
and a million maggots that had made up their brains
crawl from the empty holes and devour the flesh
that covered the evil that passed itself off as a person
that i probably tried
to love

when i die i hope every worker in the national security
      council
the interpol the fbicia foundation for the development
      of black women gets
an extra bonus and maybe takes one day off
and maybe even asks why they didn't work as hard for us
      as they did
them
but it always seems to be that way

please don't let them read "nikki-rosa" maybe just let
some black woman who called herself my friend go around
      and collect
each and every book and let some black man who said it
      was
negative of me to want him to be a man collect every
      picture
and poster and let them burn—throw acid on them—shit
      on them as
they did me while i tried
to live

and as soon as i die i hope everyone who loved me learns
    the meaning
of my death which is a simple lesson
don't do what you do very well very well and enjoy it it
    scares white folk
and makes black ones truly mad

but i do hope someone tells my son
his mother liked little old ladies with
their blue dresses and hats and gloves that sitting
    by the window
to watch the dawn come up is valid that smiling at an old
    man
and petting a dog don't detract from manhood
do
somebody please
tell him i knew all along that what would be
is what will be but i wanted to be a new person
and my rebirth was stifled not by the master
but the slave

and if ever i touched a life i hope that life knows
that i know that touching was and still is and will always
    be the true
revolution

# [Untitled]
(For Margaret Danner)


one ounce of truth benefits
like ripples on a pond
one ounce of truth benefits like a ripple
on a pond
one ounce of truth
benefits like ripples on
a pond
as things change remember my smile

the old man said my time is getting near
the old man said my time
is getting near
he looked at his dusty cracked boots to say
sister my time is getting near
and when i'm gone remember i smiled
when i'm gone remember
i smiled
i'm glad my time is getting there

the baby cried wanting some milk
the baby cried needing some milk
the baby he cried for wanting
his mother kissed him gently

when i came they sang a song
when i was born they sang a song
when i was saved they sang a song
remember i smiled when i'm gone
remember i smiled when i'm gone
sing a good song when i'm gone
we ain't got long to stay

## My Tower
(For Barb and Anthony)

i have built my tower on the wings of a spider
spinning slippery daydreams of paperdoll fantasies
i built my tower on the beak of a dove
pecking peace to a needing woman

i have built my dreams on the love of a man
holding a nation in his palm asking me the time of day

i built my castle by the shore thinking
i was an oyster clammed shut forever
when this tiny grain i hardly noticed
crept inside and i spit around
and spit around and spun a universe inside
with a black pearl of immeasurable worth
that only i could spin around

i have borne a nation on my heart
and my strength shall not be my undoing
cause this castle didn't crumble
and losing my pearl made me gain
and the dove flew with the olive branch by harriet's route
to my breast and nestled close and said "you are mine"
and i was full and complete while emptying my wombs
and the sea ebbed ohhhhhhhhh
what a pretty little baby

# Poem
(For Nina)

we are all imprisoned *in the castle of our skins*
and some of us have said so be it
if i am in jail my castle shall become
my rendezvous
my courtyard will bloom with hyacinths and jack-in-the-
    pulpits
my moat will not restrict me but will be filled
with dolphins sitting on lily pads and sea horses ridden by
    starfish
goldfish will make love
to Black mollies and color my world Black Gold
the vines entwining my windows will grow butterflies
and yellow jackets will buzz me to sleep
the dwarfs imprisoned will not become my clowns
for me to scorn but my dolls for me to praise and fuss
with and give tea parties to
my gnomes will spin cloth of spider web silkness
my wounded chocolate soldiers will sit in evening coolness
or stand gloriously at attention during that midnight sun
for i would have no need of day patrol
if i am imprisoned in my skin let it be a dark world
with a deep bass walking a witch doctor to me for spiritual
consultation
let my world be defined by my skin and the skin of my
    people
for we      spirit to spirit      will embrace
this world

## Africa I

on the bite of a kola nut
i was so high the clouds blanketing
        africa
in the mid morning flight were pushed
away in an angry flicker
of the sun's tongue

a young lioness sat smoking a pipe
while her cubs waved up at the plane
look ida i called a lion waving
but she said there are no lions
in this part of africa
it's my dream dammit i mumbled

but my grandmother stood up
from her rocker just then
and said you call it
like you see it
john brown and i are with you
and i sat back for my morning
coffee

we landed in accra and the people
clapped and i almost cried wake up
we're home

and something in me said shout
and something else said quietly
your mother may be glad to see you
but she may also remember why
you went away

# Africa II

africa is a young man bathing
in the back of a prison fortress

the guide said "are you afro-american
cape coast castle holds a lot for your people"

and the 18th century clock keeps perfect
time for the time it has

i watched his black skin turn foaming
white and wanted to see this magnificent
man stand naked and clean before me
but they called me to the dungeons where above
the christian church an african stood listening
for sounds of revolt

the lock the guide stated indicated a major once ran
the fort and the british he said had recently demanded
the lock's return
and i wanted the lock maybe for a door
stop to unstop the 18th century clock

"and there is one African buried
here     we are proud of him" he said
and i screamed NO there are thousands
but my voice was lost in the room
of the women with the secret passageway
leading to the governor's quarters

so roberta flack recorded a song
and les mccann cried but
a young african man on the rock
outside the prison where my people were
born bathed in the sunlight

and africa is a baby to be
tossed about and disciplined and loved
and neglected and bitten on its bottom
as i wanted to
sink my teeth into his thigh
and tell him he would never be
clean until he can
possess me

# They Clapped

they clapped when we landed
thinking africa was just an extension
of the black world
they smiled as we taxied home to be met
black to black face not understanding africans lack
color prejudice
they rushed to declare
cigarettes, money, allegiance to the mother land
not knowing despite having read fanon and davenport
hearing all of j.h. clarke's lectures, supporting
nkrumah in ghana and nigeria in the war that there was
    once
a tribe called afro-americans that populated the whole
of africa
they stopped running when they learned the packages
on the women's heads were heavy and that babies didn't
cry and disease is uncomfortable and that villages are fun
only because you knew the feel of good leather on good
pavement
they cried when they saw mercedes-benzes were as
    common
in lagos as volkswagens are in berlin
they shook their heads when they understood there was no
difference between the french and the english and the
    americans
and the afro-americans or the tribe next door or the country
across the border

they were exasperated when they heard sly and the family
    stone
in francophone africa and they finally smiled when little
    boys
who spoke no western tongue said "james brown" with
    reverence
they brought out their cameras and bought out africa's
    drums
when they finally realized they are strangers all over
and love is only and always about the lover not the beloved
they marveled at the beauty of the people and the richness
of the land knowing they could never possess either

they clapped when they took off
for home despite the dead
dream they saw a free future

# Poem
**(For Anna Hedgeman and Alfreda Duster)**

   thinning hair
   estee laudered
   deliberate sentences
   chubby hands
   glasses resting atop ample softness
   dresses too long
   beaded down
   elbow length gloves    funny hats
   ready smiles
       diamond rings
   hopeful questions
   needing to be needed
   my ladies over fifty
   who birthed and nursed
   my Blackness

# Atrocities

in an age of napalmed children
with words like *the enemy is whatever moves*
as an excuse for killing vietnamese infants

at a time when one president one nobel prize winner
one president's brother four to six white students
dozens of Black students and various hippies
would be corralled maimed and killed

in a day where the c.i.a. could hire Black hands to pull
the trigger on malcolm

during a decade that saw eight nurses in chicago
sixteen people at the university of texas along with
the boston stranger do a fantastic death
dance matched only by the murders of john coltrane
sonny liston jimi hendrix and janis joplin

in a technological structure where featherstone
and che would be old-fashioned bombed

at a moment when agnew could define hard and soft
drugs on the basis of his daughter's involvement
with them

in a nation where eugene robinson could testify
against his own panther recruits and eldridge cleaver

could expel a martyr from that martyr's creation
where the president who at least knows
the law would say manson who at least tried
is guilty

it is only natural that joe frazier
would emerge

# We

we stood there waiting
    on the corners
    in the bars
    on the stoops
    in the pews
    by the cadillacs
    for buses
    wanting for love
    watching to see if hope would come by
we stood there hearing
    the sound of police sirens
    and fire engines
    the explosions
    and babies crying
    the gas escaping
    and the roaches breeding
    the garbage cans falling
    and the stairways creaking
we listened
    to the books opening
    and hearts shutting
    the hands rubbing
    the bodies sweating
we were seeing the revolution screeeeeeeeeching
    to a halt
    trying to find a clever way
    to be empty

## My House

i only want to
be there to kiss you
as you want to be kissed
when you need to be kissed
where i want to kiss you
cause it's my house
and i plan to live in it

i really need to hug you
when i want to hug you
as you like to hug me
does this sound like a silly poem

i mean it's my house
and i want to fry pork chops
and bake sweet potatoes
and call them yams
cause i run the kitchen
and i can stand the heat

i spent all winter in
carpet stores gathering
patches so i could make
a quilt
does this really sound
like a silly poem
i mean i want to keep you
warm

and my windows might be dirty
but it's my house
and if i can't see out sometimes
they can't see in either

english isn't a good language
to express emotion through
mostly i imagine because people
try to speak english instead
of trying to speak through it
i don't know maybe it is
a silly poem

i'm saying it's my house
and i'll make fudge and call
it love and touch my lips
to the chocolate warmth
and smile at old men and call
that revolution cause what's real
is really real
and i still like men in tight
pants cause everybody has some
thing to give and more
important needs something to take

and this is my house and you make me
happy
so this is your poem

# The
# Women
## and the Men

# The Women Gather
(For Joe Strickland)

the women gather
because it is not unusual
to seek comfort in our hours of stress
    a man must be buried

it is not unusual
that the old bury the young
    though it is an abomination

it is not strange
that the unwise and the ungentle
carry the banner of humaneness
    though it is a castration of the spirit

it no longer shatters the intellect
that those who make war
call themselves diplomats

we are no longer surprised
that the unfaithful pray loudest
every sunday in every church
and sometimes in rooms facing east
    though it is a sin and a shame

    so how do we judge a man

most of us love from our need to love not
because we find someone deserving

most of us forgive because we have trespassed not
because we are magnanimous

most of us comfort because we need comforting
our ancient rituals demand that we give
what we hope to receive

and how do we judge a man

we learn to greet when meeting
to cry when parting
and to soften our words at times of stress

the women gather
with cloth and ointment
their busy hands bowing to laws that decree
willows shall stand swaying but unbroken
against even the determined wind of death

we judge a man by his dreams
not alone his deeds
we judge a man by his intent
not alone his shortcomings
we judge a man because it is not unusual
to know him through those who love him

the women gather strangers
to each other because
they have loved a man

it is not unusual to sift
through ashes
and find an unburnt picture

# Once A Lady Told Me

like my mother and her grandmother before
i paddle around the house
in soft-soled shoes
chasing ghosts from corners
with incense
they are such a disturbance my ghosts
they break my bric-a-brac and make
me forget to turn my heating stove

the children say you must come to live
with us     all my life i told them i've lived
with you     now i shall live with myself

the grandchildren say it's disgraceful
you in this dark house with the curtains
pulled     snuff dripping from your chin
would they be happier if i smoked     cigarettes

i was very exquisite once     very small and well courted
some would say a beauty when my hair was plaited
and i was bustled up

my children wanted my life
and now they want my death

but i shall pad around my house
in my purple soft-soled shoes
i'm very happy now
it's not so very neat, you know, but it's my
life

# Each Sunday

if she wore her dresses
the same length as mine
people would gossip viciously
about her morals

if i slept     head barely touching
the string of freshwater fake pearls
mouth slightly open     eyebrows knitted
almost into a frown
people would accuse me of running around
too much

suddenly her eyes springing away
from her sleep intensely
scope the pulpit and fall
on me

i wonder did she dream
while baking cold-water cornbread
of being a great reporter churning
all the facts together and creating
the truth
did she think     while patching the torn pants
and mending the socks of her men     of standing
arms outstretched before a great world
body offering her solution for peace
what did she feel wringing the neck
of Sunday's chicken breaking the beans
of her stifled life

she sits each sunday black
dress falling below her knees which have drifted
apart defining a void
in the temple of her life in the church of her god
strong and staunch and hopeful
that we never change
places

# The December Of My Springs

in the december of my springs
i long for the days
i shall somehow have
free from children and dinners
and people i have grown stale with

this time i think i'll face love
with my heart instead of my glands
rather than hands clutching to satiate
my fingers will stroke to satisfy
i think it might be good
to decide rather than to need

that pitter-patter rhythm of rain
sliding on city streets is as satisfying
to me as this quiet has become
and like the raindrop i accede to my nature

perhaps there will be no
difference between the foolishness of age
and the foolishness of youth
some say we are responsible
for those we love
others know we are responsible
for those who love us

so i sit waiting
for a fresh thought
to stir the atmosphere

i'm glad i'm not iron
else i would be burned
by now

# The Life I Led

i know my upper arms will grow
flabby it's true
of all the women in my family

i know that the purple veins
like dead fish in the Seine
will dot my legs one day
and my hands will wither while
my hair turns grayish white      i know that
one day my teeth will move when
my lips smile
and a flutter of hair will appear
below my nose      i hope
my skin doesn't change to those blotchy
colors

i want my menses to be undifficult
i'd very much prefer staying firm and slim
to grow old like a vintage wine fermenting
in old wooden vats with style
i'd like to be exquisite      i think

i will look forward to grandchildren
and my flowers      all my knickknacks in their places
and that quiet of the bombs not falling in cambodia
settling over my sagging breasts

i hope my shoulder finds a head that needs nestling
and my feet find a footstool after a good soaking
with epsom salts

i hope i die
warmed
by the life that i tried
to live

## The Way I Feel

i've noticed i'm happier
when i make love
with you
and have enough left
over to smile at my doorman

i've realized i'm fulfilled
like a big fat cow
who has just picked
for a carnation contentment
when you kiss your special place
right behind my knee

i'm as glad as mortar
on a brick that knows
another brick is coming
when you walk through
my door

most time when you're around
i feel like a note
roberta flack is going to sing

in my mind you're a clock
and i'm the second hand sweeping
around you sixty times an hour
twenty-four hours a day
three hundred sixty-five days a year
and an extra day
in leap year
cause that's the way
that's the way
that's the way i feel
about you

## Communication

if music is the most universal language
just think of me as one whole note

if science has the most perfect language
picture me as $MC^2$

since mathematics can speak to the infinite
imagine me as 1 to the first power

what i mean is     one day
i'm gonna grab your love
and you'll be
satisfied

# Luxury

i suppose living
in a materialistic society
luxury
to some would be having
more than what you need

living in an electronic age seeing
the whole world by pushing a button
the *nth* degree might perhaps be
adequately represented by having
someone there to push
the buttons for you

i have thought if only
i could become rich and famous i would
live luxuriously in new york knowing
famous people eating
in expensive restaurants calling
long distance anytime i want

but you held me
one evening and now i know
the ultimate luxury
of your love

# Poem

like a will-o'-the-wisp in the night
on a honeysuckle breeze
a moment sticks
us together

like a dolphin being
tickled on her stomach
my sea of love flip-flops all
over my face

like the wind blowing
across a field of wheat
your smile whispers to my inner ear

with the relief of recognition
i bend to your eyes
casually
raping me

## Hampton, Virginia

the birds flew south
earlier this year
and flowers wilted under the glare
of frost
nature puts her house in order

the weather reports say this
will be the coldest winter
already the perch have burrowed
deep into the lakes
and the snails are six instead
of three feet under

i quilted myself
one blanket and purchased five
pounds of colored popcorn
in corners i placed dried
flowers and in my bathroom a jar
of lavendar smells
my landlord stripped my windows
and i cut all my old sox for feet pads

they say you should fight the cold with the cold
but since i never do anything right
i called you

## Poetry Is a Trestle

poetry is a trestle
spanning the distance between
what i feel
and what i say

like a locomotive
i rush full speed ahead
trusting your strength
to carry me over

sometimes we share a poem
because people are near
and they would notice me
noticing you
so i write X and you write O
and we both win

sometimes we share a poem
because i'm washing the dishes
and you're looking at your news

or sometimes we make a poem
because it's Sunday and you want
ice cream while i want cookies

but always we share a poem
because belief predates action
and i believe
the most beautiful poem
ever heard is your heart
racing

# Something To Be Said For Silence

there is something
to be said for silence
    it's almost as sexual as moving
    your bowels

i wanted to be in love
when winter came
like a groundhog i would burrow
under the patchwork pieces
of your love
but the threads are slender
and they are being stretched

i guess it's all right
to want to feel
though it's better to really feel
and sometimes i wonder
did i ever love anyone

i like my house my job i gave up
my car
but i bought a new coat
and somewhere something is missing
    i do all the right things
maybe i'm just tired
maybe i'm just tired of being tired
i feel sometimes so inert
and laws of motion being what they are
i feel we won't feel again

it's all right with me
if you want to love
it's all right with me if you don't
my silence is at least
as sexy as your love
and twice as easy
to take

# Africa

i am a teller of tales
a dreamer of dreams
    shall i spin a poem around you
human beings grope to strangers
to share a smile
complain to lovers of their woes
and never touch
those who need to be touched
    may i move on
the african isn't independent
he's emancipated
and like the freedman he explores
his freedom rather than exploits
his nation
worrying more about the condition
of the women than his position in the world
    i am a dreamer of dreams
in my fantasy i see a person
not proud for pride is a collection of lions
or a magazine in washington d.c.
but a person who can be wrong and go on
or a person who can be praised and still work
but a person who can let a friend share a joy as easily
as a friend shares a sorrow
it's odd that all welcome a tale of disappointment
though few a note of satisfaction
have none of us been happy
    i am a teller of tales
i see kings and noblemen
slaves and serfs all selling
and being sold for what end
to die for freedom or live for joy
    i am a teller of tales
we must believe in each other's dreams
i'm told and i dream

of me accepting you and you accepting yourself
will that stroke the tension
between blacks and africans
i dream of truth lubricating our words
will that ease three hundred years
and i dream of black men and women walking
together side by side into a new world
described by love and bounded by difference
for nothing is the same except oppression and shame
    may i spin a poem around you
come let's step into my web
and dream of freedom together

# Swaziland

i am old and need
to remember
you are young and need
to learn
if i forget the words
will you remember the music

i hear a drum speaking of a stream
the path is crossing the stream
the stream is crossing the path
which came first the drums ask
the music is with the river

if we meet does it matter
that i took the step toward you

the words ask are you fertile
the music says let's dance

i am old and need to remember
you are young and want to learn
let's dance together
let's dance
together
let's
dance
together

# A Very Simple Wish

i want to write an image
like a log-cabin quilt pattern
and stretch it across all the lonely
people who just don't fit in
　　we might make a world
　　　if i do that

i want to boil a stew
with all the leftover folk
whose bodies are full
of empty lives
　　we might feed a world
　　　if i do that

twice in our lives
we need direction
when we are young and innocent
when we are old and cynical
but since the old refused
to discipline us
we now refuse
to discipline them
which is a contemptuous way
for us to respond
to each other

i'm always surprised
that it's easier to stick
a gun in someone's face
or a knife in someone's back
than to touch skin to skin
anyone whom we like

i should imagine if nature holds true
one day we will lose our hands
since we do no work nor make
any love
if nature is true
we shall all lose our eyes
since we cannot even now distinguish
the good from the evil

i should imagine we shall lose our souls
since we have so blatantly put them up
for sale and glutted the marketplace
thereby depressing the price

i wonder why we don't love
not some people way on
the other side of the world with strange
customs and habits
not some folk from whom we were sold
hundreds of years ago
but people who look like us
who think like us
who want to love us      why
don't we love them

i want to make a quilt
of all the patches and find
one long strong pole
to lift it up

i've a mind to build
a new world

want to play

# Night

in africa night walks
into day as quickly
as a moth is extinguished
by its desire for flame

the clouds in the caribbean carry
night like a young man
with a proud erection dripping
black dots across the blue sky
the wind a mistress of the sun howls
her displeasure at the involuntary
fertilization

but nights are white
in new york
the shrouds of displeasure
mask our fear of facing
ourselves between the lonely
sheets

# Poetry

poetry is motion graceful
as a fawn
gentle as a teardrop
strong like the eye
finding peace in a crowded room

we poets tend to think
our words are golden
though emotion speaks too
loudly to be defined
by silence

sometimes after midnight or just before
the dawn
we sit typewriter in hand
pulling loneliness around us
forgetting our lovers or children
who are sleeping
ignoring the weary wariness
of our own logic
to compose a poem
        no one understands it
it never says "love me" for poets are
beyond love
it never says "accept me" for poems seek not
acceptance but controversy
it only says "i am" and therefore
i concede that you are too

a poem is pure energy
horizontally contained
between the mind
of the poet and the ear of the reader
if it does not sing discard the ear
for poetry is song
if it does not delight discard
the heart for poetry is joy
if it does not inform then close
off the brain for it is dead
if it cannot heed the insistent message
that life is precious

which is all we poets
wrapped in our loneliness
are trying to say

*Cotton*

# Candy *On A Rainy*

# Day

## Cotton Candy On A Rainy Day

Don't look now
I'm fading away
Into the gray of my mornings
Or the blues of every night

Is it that my nails
    keep breaking
Or maybe the corn
      on my second little piggy
Things keep popping out
    on my face
        or
    of my life

It seems no matter how
I try I become more difficult
    to hold
I am not an easy woman
    to want

They have asked
    the psychiatrists    psychologists    politicians and
    social workers
What this decade will be
    known for
There is no doubt    it is
    loneliness

If loneliness were a grape
        the wine would be vintage
If it were a wood
        the furniture would be mahogany
But since it is life      it is
        Cotton Candy
                on a rainy day
The sweet soft essence
        of possibility
Never quite maturing

I have prided myself
On being in that great tradition
        albeit circus
That the show must go on
Though in my community the vernacular is
        One Monkey Don't Stop the Show

We all line up
        at some midway point
To thread our way through
        the boredom and futility
Looking for the blue ribbon and gold medal

Mostly these are seen as food labels

We are consumed by people who sing
  the same old song     STAY:

                              *as sweet as you are*
                              *in my corner*
Or perhaps                    *just a little bit longer*
But whatever you do     *don't change baby baby don't change*
Something needs to change
Everything     some say     will change
I need a change
    of pace     face     attitude and life
Though I long for my loneliness
I know I need something
Or someone
Or. . . . .


I strangle my words as easily as I do my tears
I stifle my screams as frequently as I flash my smile
  it means nothing
I am cotton candy on a rainy day
  the unrealized dream of an idea unborn


I share with the painters the desire
To put a three-dimensional picture
On a one-dimensional surface

# Introspection

she didn't like to think in abstracts
sadness happiness taking giving     all abstracts
she much preferred waxing the furniture
cleaning the shelves putting the plates away
something concrete to put her hands on
a job well done in a specific time span

her eyes were two bright shiny six guns
already cocked
prepared to go off at a moment's indiscretion
had she been a vietnam soldier or a mercenary
for Ian Smith     all the children and dogs and goodly
portions of grand old trees would have been demolished

she had lived both long and completely enough
not to be chained to truth
she was not pretty
she had no objections to the lies
lies were better than the silence that abounded
nice comfortable lies like     I need you
or     Gosh you look pretty this morning
the lies that make the lie of life real
or lies that make real life livable

she lived on the edge of an emotional abyss
or perhaps she lived in the well of a void
there were always things she wanted
like arms to hold her
eyes that understood
a friend to relax with
someone to touch
always      someone to touch
her life was a puzzle broken
into a hundred thousand little pieces
she didn't mind being emotionally disheveled
she was forever fascinated by putting the pieces
together      though most times
the center was empty

she never slept well
there wasn't a time
actually
when sleep refreshed her
perhaps it could have
but there were always dreams
or nightmares
and mostly her own acknowledgment
that she was meant to be tired

she lived
because she didn't know any better
she stayed alive
among the tired and lonely
not waiting      always wanting
needing a good night's rest

# Forced Retirement

all problems being
as personal as they are
have to be largely
of our own making

i know i'm unhappy
most of the time
nothing an overdose
of sex won't cure of course
but since i'm responsible
i barely have an average
intake

on the other hand
i'm acutely aware
there are those suffering
from the opposite affliction

some people die of obesity
while others starve to death
some commit suicide
because they are bored
others because of pressure
the new norm is as elusive
as the old

granting problems coming
from within
are no less painful
than those out of our hands
i never really do worry
about atomic destruction
of the universe
though i can be quite vexed
that Namath and Ali don't retire
my father has to
and though he's never made a million
or even hundreds of thousands
he too enjoys his work
and is good at it
but more        goes
even when he doesn't
feel like it

people fear boredom
not because they are        bored
rather more from fear
of boring
though minds are either sharp
or dull
and bodies available
or not
and there's something else
that's never wrong
though never quite right
either

i've always thought the beautiful
are as pitiful
as the ugly
but the average is no guarantee
of happiness

i've always wandered a bit
not knowing if this is a function
of creeping menopause
or incipient loneliness
i no longer correct my habits

nothing makes sense
if we are just a collection of genes
on a freudian altar to the species
i don't like those theories
telling me why i feel as i do
behaviorisms never made sense
outside feeling

i could say i am black female
and bright
in a white male mediocre world
but that hardly explains why
i sit on the beaches of st croix
feeling so abandoned

# The New Yorkers

In front of the bank building
after six o'clock the gathering
of the bag people begins

In cold weather they huddle
around newspapers
when it is freezing they get
cardboard boxes

Someone said they are all rich eccentrics
Someone is          of course          crazy

The man and his buddy moved
to the truck port
in the adjoining building
most early evenings he visits
his neighbors awaiting
the return of his friend
from points unknown to me
they seem to be a spontaneous
combustion these night people
they evaporate during the light of day
only to emerge at evening glow
as if they had never been away

I am told there are people
who live underground
in the layer between the subways
and the pipes that run them
they have harnessed the steam
to heat their corner
and cook their food
though there is no electricity
making them effectively          moles

The twentieth century has seen
    two big wars and two small ones
    the automobile and the SST
    telephones and satellites in the sky
    man on the moon and spacecraft on Jupiter
How odd to also see the people
of New York City living
in the doorways of public buildings
as if this is an emerging nation
though of course it is

Look at the old woman
who sits on 57th Street and 8th Avenue
selling pencils
I don't know where she spends the night
she sits summer and winter
snow or rain humming
some white religious song
she must weigh over 250 pounds
the flesh on her legs has stretched
like a petite pair of stockings
onto a medium frame
beyond its ability to fit
there are tears and holes
of various purples in her legs
things and stuff ooze from them
drying and running again
there is never    though    a smell
she does not ask you to buy
a pencil nor will her eyes
condemn your health
it's easy really to walk by her
unlike the man in front

of Tiffany's she holds her pencils
near her knee
you take or not
depending upon your writing needs

He on the other hand is blind and walking
his german shepherd dog
his sign says THERE
BUT FOR THE GRACE OF GOD
GOES YOU and there is a long
explanation of his condition
It's rather easy for the Tiffany shopper
to see his condition
      he is Black

Uptown on 125th Street is an old blind Black woman
she is out only in good
      weather and clothes
her house is probably spotless
as southern ladies are wont to keep house
and her wig is always on straight
      You got something for me, she called
      What do you want, I asked
      What's yo name? I know yo family
      No, you don't, I said laughing     You don't know
         anything about me
      You that Eyetalian poet ain't you? I know yo voice. I
         seen you on television

I peered closely into her eyes
    You didn't see me or you'd know I'm black
    Let me feel yo hair    if you Black    Hold down yo
        head
I did and she did
    Got something for me, she laughed
    You felt my hair    that's good luck
    Good luck is money, chile    she said
    Good luck is money

# Crutches

it's not the crutches we decry
it's the need to move forward
though we haven't the strength

women aren't allowed to need
so they develop rituals
since we all know working hands idle
the devil
women aren't supposed to be strong
so they develop social smiles
and secret drinking problems
and female lovers whom they never touch
except in dreams

men are supposed to be strong
so they have heart attacks
and develop other women
who don't know their weaknesses
and hide their fears
behind male lovers
whom they religiously touch
each saturday morning on the basketball court
it's considered a sign of health doncha know
that they take such good care
of their bodies

i'm trying to say something about the human condition
maybe i should try again

if you broke an arm or leg
a crutch would be a sign of courage
people would sign your cast
and you could bravely explain
no it doesn't hurt—it just itches
but if you develop an itch
there are no salves to cover the area
in need of attention
and for whatever guilt may mean
we would feel guilty for trying
to assuage the discomfort
and even worse for needing the aid

i really want to say something about all of us
am i shouting     i want you to hear me

emotional falls always are
the worst
and there are no crutches
to swing back on

# Boxes

i am in a box
on a tight string
subject to pop
without notice

everybody says how strong
i am

only black women
and white men
are truly free
they say

it's not difficult to see
how stupid they are

i would not reject
my strength
though its source
is not choice
but responsibility

i would not reject my light
though my wrinkles are also illuminated

something within demands
action
or words
if action is not possible

i am tired
of being boxed
muhammad ali must surely be pleased
that leon spinks relieved him

most of the time
i can't breathe
i smoke too much
to cover my fears
sometimes i pick
my nose to avoid
the breath i need

i do also do the same
injustice to my poems

i write because
i have to

# Poem

i have considered
my reluctance
to be a fear of death
there are all sorts of reasons
i don't want to die
    responsibility to family
    obligations to friends
    dreams of future greatness
i close my eyes and chant
on airplanes to calm
my fleeting heart
since we are riding on air
my will is as necessary
as the pilot's abilities
to keep us afloat

i have felt that way
about other endeavors

however do we justify
our lives
the president of the united states
says Faith not deeds will determine
our salvation
that's probably why larry flynt
a stand-in for carter
is without his insides now

i have faith      of course
in the deeds i do
and see done
one really can't hate
the act but love
the actor
only jewish theater and american politics
would even contemplate
such a contradiction

however will we survive
the seventies

i seize on little things
you can tell a lot about people
by the way they comb their hair
or the way they don't look
you in the eye

am i discussing nixon
again

he went to humphrey's funeral
and opened his house
(2.50 per head)
for the public to see
i can't decide if anita bryant
should marry carter or nixon
they both are so bad
they deserve her

there must be something fun
worth sharing

there is a split
between the jewish and black community
the former didn't mind
until the latter put a name to it

i live in a city
that has turned into a garbage can
there is no disagreement
about that
there is some question
concerning the dog dung in the streets
as opposed to the dog dung in the administration

ahhhh      but you will say
how awful of the poet
such insinuations she does make
nobody is perfect
i do      after all      have
this      well      reluctance

# A Poem Off Center

how do poets write
so many poems
my poems get decimated
in the dishes the laundry
my sister is having another crisis
the bed has to be made
there is a blizzard on the way go to the grocery store
did you go to the cleaners
then a fuse blows
a fuse always has to blow
the women soon find themselves
talking either to babies or about them
no matter how careful we are
we end up giving tips
on the latest new improved cleaner
and the lotion that will take the smell away

if you write a political poem
you're anti-semitic
if you write a domestic poem
you're foolish
if you write a happy poem
you're unserious
if you write a love poem
you're maudlin
of course the only real poem
to write
is the go to hell writing establishment poem
but the readers never know who
you're talking about which brings us back
to point one

i feel     i think     sorry for the women
they have no place to go
it's the same old story blacks
hear all the time
if it's serious a white man
would do it
when it's serious
he will
everything from writing a poem
to sweeping the streets
to cooking the food
as long as his family doesn't eat it

it's a little off center
this life we're leading
maybe i shouldn't feel sorry
for myself
but the more i understand women
the more i do

# Age

we tend to fear old age
as some sort of disorder     that can be cured
with the proper brand of aspirin
or perhaps a bit of Ben-Gay for the shoulders
it does     of course     pay to advertise

one hates the idea of the first gray hair
a shortness of breath
devastating blows to the ego
indications we are doing
what comes naturally

it's almost laughable
that we detest aging
when we first become aware
we want it
little girls of four or five push
with eyes shining brightly at gram or mommy
the lie that they are seven or eight
little girls at ten worry
that a friend has gotten her monthly
and she has not
little girls of twelve
can be socially crushed
by lack of nobs on their chests

little boys of fourteen want
to think they want
a woman
the little penis that simply won't erect
is shattering to their idea of manhood
if perhaps they get a little peach fuzz
on their faces they may survive
adolescence proving there may indeed be life
after high school
the children begin to play     older
without knowing the price is     weariness

age teaches us that our virtues
are neither virtuous nor our vices
foul
age doesn't matter     really
what frightens is mortality
it dawns upon us that we can die
at some point it occurs we surely shall

it is not death we fear
but the loss of youth
not the youth of our teens
where most of the thinking took place
somewhere between the navel and the knee
but the youth of our thirties where career
decisions were going well
and we were respected for our abilities
or the youth of our forties
where our decisions proved if not right
then not wrong either
and the house     after all     is half paid

it may simply be that work
is so indelibly tied
to age that the loss
of work brings the depression
of impending death
there are so many      too many
who have never worked
and therefore for whom death
is a constant companion
as lack of marriage
lowers divorce rates
lack of life
prevents death
the unwillingness to try
is worse than any failure

in youth our ignorance gives us courage
with age our courage gives us hope
with hope we learn that man is more
than the sum of what he does
we also are what we wish we did
and age teaches us
that even that doesn't matter

## Life Cycles

she realized
she wasn't one
of life's winners
when     she wasn't sure
life to her was some dark
dirty secret that
like some unwanted child
too late for an abortion
was to be borne
alone

she had so many private habits
she would masturbate sometimes
she always picked her nose when upset
she liked to sit with silence
in the dark
sadness is not an unusual state
for the black woman
or writers

she took to sneaking drinks
a habit which displeased her
both for its effects
and taste
yet eventually sleep
would wrestle her in triumph
onto the bed

she was nervous
when he was there
and anxious
when he wasn't
life     to her
was a crude cruel joke
played on the livers

she boxed her life
like a special private seed
planting it in her emotional garden
to see what weeds
would rise
to strangle
her

# Adulthood II

There is always something
of the child
in us that wants
a strong hand to hold
through the hungry season
of growing up

when she was a child
summer lasted forever
and christmas seemed never
to come
now her bills from easter
usually are paid
by the 4th of july
in time to buy the ribs
and corn and extra bag of potatoes
for salad

the pit is cleaned
and labor day is near
time to tarpaulin
the above ground pool

thanksgiving turkey
is no sooner soup
than the children's shoes
wear thin saying
christmas is near      again
bringing the february letters asking
"did you forget
us last month"

her life looks occasionally
as if it's owed to some
machine
and the only winning point
she musters is to tear
mutilate and twist
the cards demanding information
payment
and a review of her credit worthiness

she sits sometimes
in her cubicled desk
and recalls her mother
did the same things
what we have been given
we are now expected to return
and she smiles

# Habits

i haven't written a poem in so long
i may have forgotten how
unless writing a poem
is like riding a bike
or swimming upstream
or loving you
it may be a habit that once acquired
is never lost

but you say i'm foolish
of course you love me
but being loved of course
is not the same as being loved because
or being loved despite
or being loved

if you love me why
do i feel so lonely
and why do i always wake up alone
and why am i practicing
not having you to love
i never loved you that way

if being loved by you is accepting always
　　getting the worst
　　taking the least
　　hearing the excuse
and never being called when you say you will
then it's a habit
like smoking cigarettes
or brushing my teeth when i awake
something i do without
thinking
but something without
which i could just as well do

most habits occur
because of laziness
we overdrink
because our friends do
we overeat
because our parents think
we need more flesh
on the bones
and perhaps my worst habit
is overloving
and like most who live
to excess
i will be broken
in two
by my unwillingness
to control my feelings

but i sit writing
a poem
about my habits
which while it's not
a great poem
is mine
and some habits
like smiling at children
or giving a seat to an old person
should stay
if for no other reason
than their civilizing
influence

which is the ultimate
habit
i need
to acquire

# Gus
**(for my father)**

He always had pretty legs
Even now     though he has gotten fat
His legs have kept their shape

He swam
Some men get those legs from tennis
But he swam
In a sink-or-swim mud hole somewhere
In Alabama

When he was a young man
More than half a century ago
Talent was described by how well
A thing was done     not by whom
That is     considering
That Black men weren't considered
One achieved on merit

The fact that he is short
Was an idea late reaching his consciousness
He hustled the ball on the high school court
Well enough to win a college scholarship
Luckily for me
Since that's where he met my mother

I have often tried to think lately
When I first met him
I don't remember
He was a stranger
As Black or perhaps responsible fathers
Are wont to be

He worked three jobs     a feat
Without precedence though not unknown
In the hills of West Virginia or the Red Clay of Georgia
What happens to a dream
When it must tunnel under
Langston says it might explode
It might also just die
Shriveling to the here and now
Confusing the dreamer til he no longer knows
Whether he is awake or asleep

Before we ourselves:
    Meet the man
    Lie to the bill collectors
    Don't know where the mortgage payment is coming
        from
It's difficult to understand
A weakness

Before our mettle is tested
We easily consider ourselves strong
Before we see our children want
Not elaborate things
But a christmas bike or easter shoes
It's easy to say
what should have been done

Before we see our own possibility shrink
Back into the unclonable cell
From which dreams spring
It's easy to condemn

If the first sign of spring is the swallows
Then the first sign of maturity is the pride
We gulp when we realize
There are few choices in life
That are clear
Seldom is good pitted against evil
Or even better against best
Mostly it's bad versus worse
And while some may intone
        life is not fair
"Choice" by definition implies
Equally attractive alternatives
Or mutually exclusive experiences

Boxers protect themselves from blows
        with heavily greased shoulders
Football players wear helmets
Joggers have specially made shoes
        to absorb the shocks
The problem with the Life game
For unprotected players
Is not what you don't have
But what you can't give
Though ultimately there is the understanding
That even nothing is something
As long as you are there
To give the nothing     personally

Black men grow inverse
To the common experience

He grew younger as his children left home
He has both time and money to buy
The toys he never had
Lawn mowers    saws    garden equipment    CBs
    Stereos
Whatever is new and exciting
He smiles more often too
And his legs are still
quite exceptional
For a Grandfather

# Choices

if i can't do
what i want to do
then my job is to not
do what i don't want
to do

it's not the same thing
but it's the best i can
do

if i can't have
what i want     then
my job is to want
what i've got
and be satisfied
that at least there
is something more
to want

since i can't go
where i need
to go     then i must     go
where the signs point
though always understanding
parallel movement
isn't lateral

when i can't express
what i really feel
i practice feeling
what i can express
and none of it is equal
i know
but that's why mankind
alone among the mammals
learns to cry

# Photography

the eye we are told
is a camera
but the film is the heart
not the brain
and our hands joining
those that reach
develop the product

it's easy sitting in the sun
to forget that cold exists
let alone envelops
the lives of people
it's easy sitting in the sun
to forget the ice and ravages
of winter yet
there are those who would have
no other season
it's always easy when thinking
we have the best to assume
others covet it
yet surf or sea each has
its lovers and its meaning
for love

watching the red sun bleed
into the ocean
one thinks of the beauty that fire brings
if the eye is a camera and the film is the heart
then the photo assistant is god

# The Beep Beep Poem

I should write a poem
but there's almost nothing
that hasn't been said
and said and said
beautifully, ugly, blandly
excitingly
    stay in school
    make love not war
    death to all tyrants
    where have all the flowers gone
and don't they understand at kent state
the troopers will shoot . . . again

i could write a poem
because i love walking
in the rain
and the solace of my naked
body in a tub of warm water
cleanliness may not be next
to godliness but it sure feels
good

i wrote a poem
for my father but it was so constant
i burned it up
he hates change
and i'm baffled by sameness

i composed a ditty
about encore american and worldwide news
but the editorial board
said no one would understand it
as if people have to be tricked
into sensitivity
though of course they do

i love to drive my car
hours on end
along back country roads
i love to stop for cider and apples and acorn squash
three for a dollar
i love my CB when the truckers talk
and the hum of the diesel in my ear
i love the aloneness of the road
when I ascend descending curves
the power within my toe delights me
and i fling my spirit down the highway
i love the way i feel
when i pass the moon and i holler to the stars
i'm coming through

Beep Beep

# Woman

she wanted to be a blade
of grass amid the fields
but he wouldn't agree
to be the dandelion

she wanted to be a robin singing
through the leaves
but he refused to be
her tree

she spun herself into a web
and      looking for a place to rest
turned to him
but he stood straight
declining to be her corner

she tried to be a book
but he wouldn't read

she turned herself into a bulb
but he wouldn't let her grow

she decided to become
a woman
and though he still refused
to be a man
she decided it was all
right

# Poem (for EMA)

though i do wonder
why you intrigue me
i recognize that an exceptional moth
is always drawn
to an exceptional flame

you're not at all what you appear
to be
though not so very different

i've not learned
the acceptable way of saying
you fascinate me
I've not even learned
how to say i like you
without frightening people
away

sometimes I see things
that aren't really there
like warmth and kindness
when people are mean
but sometimes i see things
like fear and want to soothe it
or fatigue and want to share it
or love and want to receive it

is that weird
you think everyone is weird
though you're not really hypocritical
you just practice not being
what you want to be
and fail to understand
how others would dare
to be otherwise
that's weird to me

flames don't flicker
forever
and moths are born to be burned

it's an unusual way
to start a friendship
but nothing lasts forever

# The Rose Bush
**(for Gordon)**

i know i haven't grown but
i don't fit beneath the rose
bush by my grandmother's porch

i couldn't have grown so much though
i don't see why the back of the couch
doesn't hide me from my sister

the lightning that would flash
on summer days brought shouts
of you children be still    the lightning's
gonna get you

we laughed my cousins and sister and i
at the foolish old people
and their backward superstitions
though lightning struck me
in new york city
and i ran
to or from what    i'm not sure
but i was hit
and now i don't fit
beneath the rose bushes
anymore
anyway    they're gone

# Patience

there are sounds
which shatter
the staleness of lives
transporting the shadows
into the dreams

raindrops falling
on leaves shatter
the dust of the city
as soap washed off
bodies shatters
the complacent dirt

she waited for him
to take away that quiet

she waited for his call
with the patience of a slave
woman quilting or a jewish mother
simmering chicken broth

there would be no other
sound than his voice
to shatter the quiet
of her heart

she waited for him
to come

# Make Up

we make up our faces
for lots of reasons
to go to the movies
or some junior prom
to see ice hockey
or watch the Dodgers come home again
defeated

going to the grocery store
only requires lipstick
while a bridge game
can mean a quick trip
to the hairdresser for a touch up

i clean my make up
before going to bed
alone
and if my mood is foul
i spray the sheets
with Ultra Ban

most faces are made up
before the public is faced
whether male female or child
it's always so appropriate
doncha know
to put a little mascara
around the eyes

we make up fantasies
to face life
we need to believe
we are good on the job
or at least in the bed

we make up lies
to impress people
who are making up lies
to impress us
and if either took all
the make up off
life would not be
worth living

we make up excuses
to say i'm sorry *that*
forgive me *because*
and after all didn't i tell you
*why*

and i make up with you
because you aren't strong
enough to reach out
to say
come home     i need you

## Winter

Frogs burrow the mud
snails bury themselves
and I air my quilts
preparing for the cold

Dogs grow more hair
mothers make oatmeal
and little boys and girls
take Father John's Medicine

Bears store fat
chipmunks gather nuts
and I collect books
For the coming winter

# You Are There

i shall save my poems
for the winter of my dreams
i look forward to huddling
in my rocker with my life
i wonder what i'll contemplate
lovers—certainly those
i can remember
and knowing my life
you'll be there

you'll be there in the cold
like a Siamese on my knee
proud purring when you let me stroke you

you'll be there in the rain
like an umbrella over my head
sheltering me from the damp mist

you'll be there in the dark
like a lighthouse in the fog
seeing me through troubled waters

you'll be there in the sun
like coconut oil on my back
to keep me from burning

i shall save a special poem
for you to say
you always made me smile
and even though i cried sometimes
you said i will not let you
down

my rocker and i on winter's porch
will never be sad if you're gone
the winter's cold has been stored
against
you will always be
there

## Turning (I need a better title)

she often wondered why people spoke
of gaining years as turning
when she celebrated her thirtieth birthday she knew
she had turned though
she hadn't gained

the rain turned on her windowsill
and it didn't gain
and he like her face gaining
wrinkles
turned indifferent

she became happier without
the big apartment
the stereo components
and the ten pounds she shed
while adjusting to the loss
of his love

her fault lay
in her honesty
it was always his sexiness
that held her not
his arms
it was his lovemaking not
his love she missed

she compacted her
life into one
tiny room with kitchen     bed and roaches
in the four corners which contained nothing
that couldn't be stolen
or left in case
she had to run
for her sanity

so she turned thirty-one
with all
the introspections that nothing
not even them was meant
not to turn
and from that understanding
she gained
knowledge

# A Poem of Friendship

We are not lovers
because of the love
we make
but the love
we have

We are not friends
because of the laughs
we spend
but the tears
we save

I don't want to be near you
for the thoughts we share
but the words we never have
to speak

I will never miss you
because of what we do
but what we are
together

# Being and Nothingness
*(to quote a philosopher)*


i haven't done anything
meaningful in so long
it's almost meaningful
to do nothing

i suppose i could fall in love
or at least in line
since i'm so discontented
but that takes effort
and i don't want to exert anything
neither my energy nor my emotions

i've always prided myself
on being a child of the sixties
and we are all finished
so that makes being
nothing

# The Moon Shines Down

the moon shines down
on new york city
while i smile over
at you

the moon is still
against the night
and i am still
against you

surely you must sometimes wonder
won't i ever go home
surely you must sometimes say
poet please leave me alone

but my bad rhyme
and love of night
retain me here with you
and though it's so sad to admit
without you what would i do

of course you are no panacea
for my lack of friends
but if i were a hallmark card
here's where we'd begin

    the moon shines down
    on new york city
    while i smile over
    at you

# That Day

if you've got the key
then i've got the door
let's do what we did
when we did it before

if you've got the time
i've got the way
let's do what we did
when we did it all day

you get the glass
i've got the wine
we'll do what we did
when we did it overtime

if you've got the dough
then i've got the heat
we can use my oven
til it's warm and sweet

i know i'm bold
coming on like this
but the good things in life
are too good to be missed

now time is money
and money is sweet
if you're busy baby
we can do it on our feet

we can do it on the floor
we can do it on the stair
we can do it on the couch
we can do it in the air

we can do it in the grass
and in case we get an itch
i can scratch it with my left hand
cause i'm really quite a witch

if we do it once a month
we can do it in time
if we do it once a week
we can do it in rhyme
if we do it every day
we can do it everyway
we can do it like we did it
when we did it
that day

# Those

*Who Ride the*

*Night* **Winds**

# Charting the Night Winds

The first poem ... ever written ... was probably carved ... on a cold damp cave ... by a physically unendowed cave man ... who wanted to make a good impression ... on a physically endowed ... cave woman ... But maybe not ... Maybe it was she ... trying to gain the notice ... of a hunk ... who was in demand ... Or perhaps ... it was simply someone ... who admired the motion ... of a sabertooth tiger ... and wanting to capture the beauty ... picked up a sharpened rock ... to draw ... We know so very little ... about the origin of the written word ... let alone the language ... that all conjecture deserves some consideration ...

The fears ... of the human race ... are legion ... Perhaps our size ... strength ... and speed ... coupled with our ability ... to see our weakness ... have made us an anxious species ... There are smaller mammals ... There are more vulnerable life-forms ... Yet we alone can give vent to our understanding ... of the tenuousness of Life ...

Nature is a patient teacher ... She slowly changes ... winter to summer ... by proper use ... of spring and fall ... That's kind ... of nature ... Humans fear ... sudden change ... Hurricanes ... Volcanoes ... Earthquakes ... Tornadoes ... all are generally perceived ... as aberrant ... Blizzards ... in winter ... Electrical storms ... in summer ... are a part of the season ... But change ... both gradual ... and violent ... is a necessary ingredient ... with Life ...

Art ... and by necessity ... artists ... are on the cutting edge ... of change ... The very fact ... that something has been done ... over and over again ... is one reason ... to change ... Everything ... must change ... if only through perception ... Honor thy Father and Mother ... does not change ... though the understanding of long life has ... Do unto others as you would have them do unto you ... has not changed ...

though the application must move from the individual to the nation . . . What goes up must come down . . . will not change . . . though our rock stars and superathletes seem impervious . . . to the lessons of Telstar . . . There is . . . in reality . . . very little that is new . . . under the yellow sun . . . We have only rearranged the matter . . . and reconceptualized the thought . . . Greed . . . is a terrible thing . . . Envy . . . is not an acceptable emotion . . . Jealousy . . . is dangerous to your emotional life . . . and the physical and mental well-being . . . of your loved one . . . Though people say . . . they cannot change . . . change we do . . . in our abilities . . . desires . . . understanding . . . The need to force . . . humans to change . . . may be one reason we all grow . . . older . . . though there is no corresponding gene . . . to make us grow . . . wiser . . .

In the written arts . . . language has opened . . . becoming more accessible . . . more responsive . . . to what people really think . . . and say . . . We are now free . . . to use any profane word . . . or express any profound thought . . . we may wish . . . Sexuality . . . once a great taboo in language . . . and act . . . is fully explored . . . through fiction . . . and nonfiction . . . through poetry . . . and plays . . . Different and same gender . . . different and same age . . . different and same race . . . religion . . . or creed . . . all take their places . . . on the bookshelves . . . Ideas that once allowed the State to poison Socrates . . . Ideas that once allowed the Church to force Galileo to recant . . . Ideas that once encouraged McCarthy to destroy the lives of men and women . . . are now as acceptable as a stop-and-go light . . . or at least as well understood . . . as fluoride . . . While there is surely much . . . to be done . . . some change has rent . . . its ways . . . I changed . . . I chart the night winds . . . glide with me . . . I am the walrus . . . the time has come . . . to speak of many things . . .

# Lorraine Hansberry:

*An Emotional View*

It's intriguing to me that "bookmaker" is a gambling . . . an underworld . . . term somehow associated with that which is both illegal . . . and dirty . . . Bookmakers . . . and those who play with them . . . are dreamers . . . are betting on a break . . . a lucky streak . . . that something will come . . . their way— something good . . . something clean . . . something wonderful . . . We who make books . . . we who write our dreams . . . confess our fears . . . and witness our times are not so far . . . from the underworld . . . are not so far . . . from illegality . . . are not so far from the root . . . the dirt . . . the heart of the matter.

Writers . . . I think . . . live on that fine line between insanity and genius . . . Either scaling the mountains . . . or skirting the valleys . . . Riding that lonely train of truth . . . with just enough of the player in us . . . to continue to hope . . . for the species . . . Writers are . . . perhaps . . . congenital hypocrites . . . I don't think preachers . . . priests . . . rabbis . . . and ayatollahs are hypocritical . . . because they have tubular vision . . . are indeed . . . myopic . . . They know the answer . . . before you ask the question . . . But the writer . . . the painter . . . the sculptor . . . the creator . . . those who work . . . with both the mind . . . and the heart of mankind . . . have no reason . . . to be hopeful . . . We have . . . in fact . . . no right to write the happy ending . . . or the love poem . . . no reason . . . to sculpt David . . . or paint . . . like Charles White . . . We who have seen . . . all sides of the coin . . . the front . . . the back . . . and the ribbed edge . . . know what the ending . . . will surely be . . . Yet we speak . . . to and of . . . courage . . . love . . . hope . . . something better . . . in mankind . . . When we are perfectly honest . . . with ourselves . . . we cannot justify . . . our faith . . . Yet faith we do have . . . and continue to share.

Bookmaking is shooting craps . . . with the white boys . . . downtown on the stock exchange . . . is betting a dime you can win . . . a hundred . . . Making books is shooting craps . . . with God . . . is wandering into a casino where you don't even know the language . . . let alone the rules of the game . . . And that's proper . . . that's as it should be . . . If you wanted to be safe . . . you would have walked into the Post Office . . . or taken a graduate degree in Educational Administration . . . If you want to share . . . a vision . . . or tell the truth . . . you pick up . . . your pen . . . And take your chances . . . This is not . . . after all . . . tennis . . . where sets can be measured by points . . . or football . . . where games run on time . . . or baseball . . . where innings structure the play . . . It is life . . . open-ended . . . And once the play has begun . . . the book made . . . time . . . is the only judge.

Time . . . to the Black American . . . has always been . . . a burden . . . from 1619 to now . . . we have played out our drama . . . before a reluctant time . . . We were either too late . . . or too early . . . No people on Earth . . . in all her history . . . has ever produced so many people . . . so generally considered . . . "ahead of their time." . . . From the revolts in Africa . . . to our kidnapping . . . to the martyrs of freedom today . . . our people have been burdened . . . by someone else's sense . . . of the appropriate . . . There are . . . of course . . . all the jokes . . . about C. P. time . . . and there are the reminders . . . by the keepers of our souls . . . that God "is never late . . . but He always comes . . . on time." . . . To be Black . . . in America . . . is to not at all understand . . . time . . . Little Linda Brown was told . . . her school would be desegregated . . . "with all deliberate speed" . . . and twenty-five years later . . . this is still . . . untrue . . . Dr. King was told . . . in Montgomery . . . he was pushing too hard . . . going too fast . . . expecting too much . . . I wish we had been enslaved . . . at the same rate we are being set . . . free . . . It would be . . . an entirely different story . . . I wish the battleships . . . had sailed down the Mississippi River . . . when Emmett Till was lynched . . . at the same speed they sped to Cuba . . . during the missile crisis . . . I wish food . . . had been airlifted . . . to the sharecroppers in Tennessee . . . when they were pushed off the land . . . for exercising their right to vote . . . at the same speed . . . it was airlifted . . . to West Berlin . . . at the ending of World War II . . . But I'm only a colored poet . . . and my wishes . . . no matter which star I choose . . . do not come true . . . But I'm also a writer . . . and I know . . . that the Europeans aren't the only ones . . . who keep time . . . some of the time is going . . . to be my time . . . too . . .

Life teaches us not to regret . . . not to spend too much time on what might have been . . . It is neither emotionally . . . nor intellectually possible . . . for me to dwell on might-have-beens . . . I have a great love of history and antiques . . . the past is there to instruct us . . . I am socially retarded . . . so I hold on . . . to old friends . . . I like to be surrounded . . . by that which is warm and familiar . . . yet I'm sorry . . . I never met Lorraine Hansberry . . . I vividly understand that a writer is not the book she made . . . any more than a child is the print of his parents . . . Many of us are personally paranoid . . . generally uncommunicative . . . and basically unnice . . . just like most people . . . But I think Lorraine must have been one . . . of those wonderful humans who . . . seeing both sides of the dilemma . . . and all sides of the coin . . . still called "Heads" . . . when she tossed . . . And in her gamble . . . never came up snake eyes . . . It's not that she wrote . . . beautifully . . . and truthfully . . . though she did . . . It's not just that she anticipated . . . our people and their reactions . . . though she did . . . She also . . . when reading through . . . and between the lines . . . possessed that quality of courage . . . to say what had to be said . . . to those who needed to hear it . . . If writers are visionary . . . her ministry was successful . . . She made it . . . possible for all of us . . . to look . . . a little . . . deeper.

# Hands: For Mother's Day

I think hands must be very important... Hands: plait hair ... knead bread ... spank bottoms ... wring in anguish ... shake the air in exasperation ... wipe tears, sweat, and pain from faces ... are at the end of arms which hold ... Yes hands ... Let's start with the hands ...

My grandmother washed on Mondays ... every Monday ... If you were a visiting grandchild or a resident daughter ... every Monday morning at 6:00 A.M. ... mostly in the dark ... frequently in the cold ... certainly alone ... you heard her on the back porch starting to hum ... as Black Christian ladies are prone to do ... at threshold ... some plea to higher beings for forgiveness and the power to forgive ...

I saw a photograph once of the mother of Emmett Till ... a slight, brown woman with pillbox hat ... white gloves ... eyes dark beyond pain ... incomprehensibly looking at a world that never intended to see her son be a man ... That same look is created each year ... without the hat and gloves, for mother seals are not chic ... at the Arctic Circle ... That same look is in vogue in Atlanta, Cincinnati, Buffalo ... for much the same reason ... During one brief moment, for one passing wrinkle in time, Nancy Reagan wore that look ... sharing a bond, as yet unconsummated ... with Betty Shabazz, Jacqueline Kennedy, Coretta King, Ethel Kennedy ... The wives and mothers are not so radically different ... It is the hands of the women which massage the balm ... the ointments ... the lotions into the bodies for burial ... It is our hands which: cover the eyes of small children ... soothe the longing of the brothers ... make the beds ... set the tables ... wipe away our own grief ... to give comfort to those beyond comfort ...

I yield from women whose hands are Black and rough ... The women who produced me are in defiance of Porcelana and Jergens lotion . . . are ignorant of Madge's need to soak their fingernails in Palmolive dishwashing liquid . . . My women look at cracked . . . jagged fingernails that will never be adequately disguised by Revlon's new spring reds . . . We of the unacceptably strong take pride in the strength of our hands . . .

Some people think a quilt is a blanket stretched across a Lincoln bed . . . or from frames on a wall . . . a quaint museum piece to be purchased on Bloomingdale's 30-day same-as-cash plan . . . Quilts are our mosaics . . . **Michelle-Angelo's** contribution to beauty . . . We weave a quilt with dry, rough hands . . . Quilts are the way our lives are lived . . . We survive on patches . . . scraps . . . the leftovers from a materially richer culture . . . the throwaways from those with emotional options . . . We do the far more difficult job of taking that which nobody wants and not only loving it . . . not only seeing its worth . . . but making it lovable . . . and intrinsically worthwhile . . .

Though trite . . . it's nonetheless true . . . that a little knowledge is a dangerous thing . . . Perhaps pitiful thing would be more accurate . . . though that too is not profound . . . The more we experience the human drama . . . the more we are to understand . . . that whatever is not quite well about us will also not quite go away . . .

Sometimes . . . when it's something like Mother's Day . . . you really do wish you were smart enough to make the pain stop . . . to make the little hurts quit throbbing . . . to share with Star Trek's Spock the ability to touch your fingertips to the temples and make all the dumb . . . ugly . . . sad things of this world ease from memory . . . It's not at all that we fail to forgive others for the hurts we have received . . . we cannot forgive ourselves for the hurts we have meted . . . So . . . of course . . . we use our hands to push away rather than to pull closer . . .

We look . . . in vain . . . for an image of mothers . . . for an analogy for families . . . for a reason to continue . . . We live . . . mostly because we don't know any better . . . as best we can . . . Some of us are lucky . . . we learn to like ourselves . . . to forgive ourselves . . . to care about others . . . Some of us . . . on special occasions . . . watch the ladies in the purple velvet house slippers with the long black dresses come in from Sunday worship and we realize **man** never stood up to catch and kill prey . . . **man** never reared up on his hind legs to free his front parts to hold weapons . . . WOMAN stood to free her hands . . . to hold her young . . . to embrace her sons and lovers . . . WOMAN stood to applaud and cheer a delicate mate who needs her approval . . . WOMAN stood to wipe the tears and sweat . . . to touch the eyes and lips . . . that woman stood to free the arms which hold the hands . . . which hold.

# This Is Not for John Lennon

*(and this is not a poem)*

Not more than we can bear . . . more than we should have to
. . . Those of us lacking the grace to kill ourselves take it in
the gut . . . from a gun or gossip . . . what's the difference . . .
Anything in the name of the Lord . . . or Freud . . . and don't
forget the book contracts and possible made-for-TV-movies
starring that cute little buttoned-down guy who you recently
saw making some sort of deal with a game show host . . . It's
bad form to point out that Jesus didn't wear no shoes nor
carry any guns and wasn't even known to have a choice on
the presidential preference poll (though His father was
quoted a lot) . . . He has been seen however a lot at football
games cheering the Catholic teams on to victory . . . let us
all be born just one more time . . . we may yet get it . . .
right . . .

Something's wrong and this is not a poem . . . the main dif-
ference being that you didn't think it was . . . Unlike those
who profess to be caring and Christian I didn't fool you . . .
it's not about John Lennon either . . . he's dead . . . And the
man who killed him is cutting a deal . . . with doctors whose
only operations are with lawyers over how to split the money
and the 15 minutes of fame Andy Warhol so solemnly prom-
ised . . . What a pitiful country this is . . . Our beloved mayor
who prefers capital punishment to Jesus as a foolish belief all
of a sudden defends the violence of New York by saying,
"But golly gee fellows there is violence in England too" . . .
Yes indeedy folks it's not the gun but the man . . . Maybe the
New Right is finally right about something . . . Let's ban the
men . . . Let's make them justify their existence and their
right to survival . . . Let us set up a board . . . a bureaucracy
even . . . where each one must come in and fill out in tripli-
cate the reasons why he should be allowed to live . . . All po-
tential suicides need not bother to apply . . . They can save
us all grief by killing them real selves instead of they play
selves . . . Strange isn't it if you try to live by getting a job or

creating one there is no help ... If you try to die by drugs or pills or slicing your wrists you become very very significant ... No ... Not more than we can bear ... more than we ought to ...

But those who ride the night winds must learn to love the stars ... those who live on the edge must get used to the cuts ... We are told if we live in glass houses to neither throw nor stow the stones ... We are warned of bric-a-brac that easily breaks ... IF YOU BREAK IT YOU BOUGHT IT ... the store sign says ... science being such a tenuous commodity we can only half believe for every action there is an equal and opposite reaction ... But if Newton was as correct about apples as the snake we are at the beginning not the end ... Those who have nothing to offer take something away ... Don't cry for John Lennon cry for ourselves ... He was an astronaut of inner space ... He celebrated happiness ... soothed the lonely ... braced the weary ... gave word to the deaf ... vision to the insensitive ... sang a long low note when he reached the edge of this universe and saw the Blackness ... Poetry ... like photography ... functions best not only in the available light but in the timeliness of the subject ... There are always those painters who think the only proper subjects are those who can rent the galleries ... Others know we who cut stone must envision cathedrals ... I don't believe you know someone just because you like what they do for a living ... or the product of it ... You don't feel you know David Rockefeller and you all like money ... or what it can buy ... You don't feel you know or want to know Jerry Falwell and you all want to go to heaven ... or so you say ... No this is not about John Lennon ... He only wrote and sang some songs ... So did Chuck Willis ... Johnny Ace ... Sam Cooke ... Otis Redding ... The blood on city streets and backcountry roads isn't new ... but now we can call this game exactly what it is ... This isn't about somebody who killed ... either ... It's always a nut though isn't it ... cashew ... peanut ... walnut ... pistachio ... yeah ... a real pissedaschio nut ... But take comfort music lovers ... Reagan supports gun control ... ling freaks ... And those who ride the night winds do learn to love the stars ... even while crying in the darkness ... The whole may be greater than the sum of its parts ... we'll never know now ... one part is missing ... No this is not about John Lennon ... It's about us ... And the night winds ... Anybody want a ticket to ride?

# Mirrors
*(for Billie Jean King)*

The face in the window ... is not the face in the mirror ...
Mirrors aren't for windows ... they would block the light ...
Mirrors are for bedroom walls ... or closet doors ... Windows
show who we hope to be ... Mirrors reflect who we are ...
Mirrors ... like religious fervors ... are private ... and actu-
ally uninteresting to those not involved ... Windows open up
... bring a fresh view ... windows make us vulnerable

The French teach us in love ... there is always one who
kisses ... and one who offers ... the cheek ... There is many
a slip ... 'twixt the cup and the lip ... that's the reason ...
napkins were born ... In love ... there is always the hurt ...
and the hurter ... even when the hurter doesn't want ... to
hurt ... the hurtee selfishly strikes

Lips ... like brownish gray gulls infested by contact with
polluted waters circling a new jersey garbage heap ... flap in
anticipation
Lips ... like an old pot-bellied unshaven voyeur with the
grease of his speciality packed under his dirty ragged finger-
nails ... move with the glee of getting a good lick in
Lips ... like a blind man describing an elephant by touch
... give inadequate information

There are things ... that we know ... yet don't want to see
... NOT THINGS ... like abused children ... that is public
pain ... and light must be focused ... to bring the healing
heat ... NOT THINGS ... like battered wives ... that is
public policy ... if we allow silence to cover the cries ...
NOR THINGS ... like the emotionally troubled ... only
Dick and Jane ... or Ozzie and Harriet ... are always smiling
... NOT THINGS ... like people in wheelchairs ... who
need sidewalk access ... NOR THINGS ... like the un-
sighted ... who need braille in public elevators ... BUT
THINGS ... like love ... and promises made after midnight

...the rituals and responsibilities of courtship...have no place...in the court yard...are not a part of the public see ...Pillow Talk is only a movie starring Doris Day or a song by Sylvia...something delightful if you're lucky...or necessary if you're needy...but always private...since you're human

The hands of children break...drinking glasses...dinner plates...wooden buses...dolls with long blond hair... Lego structures...down...While playing blind man's bluff ...flower heads and beds suffer little gym-toed carelessness ...When playing kickball...baseball...football...soccer ...windows unshuttered shatter...it's only natural...they are children...Childish adults want to break mirrors... want to shatter lives...While eating and playing paraphernalia are easily replaced...toys forgotten...flowers regrown ...windows quickly repaired...sometimes with a scolding/ sometimes with a shrug...mirrors broken...promise seven years...bad luck...Like Humpty Dumpty...lives... once exposed to great heights...seem destined...for great falls...and are seldom properly repaired

Some people choose heroes...because they kiss a horse... and ride...alone...into the sunset...Some choose a hero ...because he robbed the rich...and gave to the poor... Some want to emulate lives...that discovered cures for exotic diseases...or made a lot of money off foolish endeavors...One of my heroes...is a tennis player...who has the courage of her game...and her life..."It Was A Mistake" for sure...if courtship turns to courts...if letters written to share a feeling come back...to testify against you ..."It Was A Mistake" to choose the myopic...selfish... greedy as a repository of a feeling..."It Was A Mistake" to want that which does not want you but what you can do...

but It Cannot Be A Mistake to have cared . . . It Cannot Be
An Error to have tried . . . It Cannot Be Incorrect to have
loved

It is illogical to spit . . . upon a face you once kissed
It is mean . . . to blacken eyes . . . which once beheld you
It is wrong . . . to punish the best . . . within

One of my heroes embraced . . . Medusa . . . but the mirror
will not break . . . it only shattered . . . The window did not
crack . . . it only opened . . . I am not ashamed . . . only sad . . .
not for my hero . . . but for those who fail to see . . . the true
championship . . . match

# Linkage
*(for Phillis Wheatley)*

What would a little girl think . . . boarding a big . . . at least to her . . . ship . . . setting sail on a big . . . to everybody . . . ocean . . . Perhaps seeing her first . . . iceberg . . . or whale . . . or shark . . . Watching the blue water kiss . . . the blue sky . . . and blow white clouds . . . to the horizon . . . My mother . . . caused awe . . . in me for blowing . . . smoke rings . . . What would a little girl think . . . leaving Senegal . . . for that which had no name . . . and when one was obtained . . . no place for her . . .

You see them now . . . though they were always . . . there . . . the children of Hester Prynne . . . walking the streets . . . needing a place . . . to eat . . . sleep . . . Be . . . warm . . . loved . . . alone . . . together . . . complete . . . The block . . . that little Black girls . . . stood upon . . . is the same block . . . they now walk . . . with little white boys and girls . . . selling themselves . . . to the adequate . . . bidder . . .

Hagar was a little Black girl . . . chosen by Sarah and Abraham . . . looked like a breeder . . . they said . . . Phillis . . . a little Black girl . . . chosen by Wheatley . . . looked intelligent . . . make a cute pet . . . for the children . . . Old men . . . sweat curling round their collars . . . choose a body and act . . . on the wait . . . through the tunnel to Jersey . . . Looked like fun . . . they say . . . Family members . . . and family friends . . . inhale to intoxication . . . the allure of the youths . . . destroying in conception . . . that which has never been . . . born . . .

Eyes . . . they say . . . are the mirror . . . of the soul . . . a reflection . . . of the spirit . . . an informer . . . to reality . . . What do you see . . . if you are a little Black girl . . . standing on a stage . . . waiting to be purchased . . . Is there kindness . . . concern . . . compassion . . . in the faces examining you . . . Do your eyes show . . . or other eyes acknowledge . . . that you . . . dusky . . . naked of clothes and tongue . . . stripped of the

protection of Gods . . . and countrymen . . . are Human . . . Do
you see those who purchase . . . or those who sold . . . Do you
see those who grab at you . . . or those who refused to shield
you . . . Are you grateful to be bought . . . or sold . . . What
would you think . . . of a people . . . who allowed . . . nay en-
couraged . . . abetted . . . regaled . . . in your chains . . . Hands
. . . that handle heavy objects . . . develop callouses . . . Feet in
shoes too tight . . . develop corns . . . Minds that cannot com-
prehend . . . like lovers separated too long . . . develop an af-
finity for what is . . . and an indifference . . . if not hostility . . .
to that which has been denied . . . Little white boys . . . stalk-
ing Park Avenue . . . little white girls . . . on the Minnesota
Strip . . . are also slaves . . . to the uncaring . . . of a nation . . .

It cannot be unusual . . . that the gene remembers . . . It di-
vides . . . and redivides . . . and subdivides . . . again and again
and again . . . to make the eyes brown . . . the fingers long . . .
the hair coarse . . . the nose broad . . . the pigment Black . . .
the mind intelligent . . . It cannot be unusual . . . that one gene
. . . from all the billions upon billions . . . remembered clitorec-
tomies . . . infibulations . . . women beaten . . . children hun-
gry . . . garbage heaping . . . open sewers . . . men laughing . . .
at it all . . . It cannot be unusual . . . that the dark . . . dusky . . .
murky world . . . of druggery . . . drums . . . witch doctors . . .
incantations . . . MAGIC . . . was willingly shed . . . for the En-
lightenment . . . At least man . . . was considered rational . . .
At least books . . . dispensed knowledge . . . At least God . . .
though still angry and jealous . . . was reachable through
prayer and action . . . if those are not redundant . . . terms . . .
We cannot be surprised that young Phillis chose poetry . . . as
others choose prostitution . . . to express her dismay . . .

The critics . . . from a safe seat in the balcony . . . disdain her
performance . . . reject her reality . . . ignore her truths . . .
How could she . . . they ask . . . thank God she was brought . . .

and bought . . . in this Land . . . How dare she . . . they decried
. . . cheer George Washington his victory . . . Why couldn't she
. . . they want to know . . . be more like . . . more like . . . more
like . . . The record sticks . . . Phillis was her own precedent
. . . her own image . . . her only ancestor . . . She wasn't like
Harriet Tubman because she is Tubman . . . with Pen . . .
rather than body . . . Leading herself . . . and therefore her
people . . . from bondage . . . not like Sojourner Truth . . . she
was Truth . . . using words on paper . . . to make the case . . .
that slavery is people . . . and wrong to do . . . We know noth-
ing of the Life . . . we who judge others . . . of the conditions
. . . we create . . . and expect others to live with . . . or beyond
. . . broken spirits . . . broken hearts . . . misplaced love . . .
fruitless endeavor . . . Women . . . are considered complete . . .
when they marry . . . We have done . . . it is considered . . . our
duty . . . when we safely deliver a person from the bondage of
Father . . . to the bondage of duty . . . and husband . . . from
house slaves who read and write . . . to housewives who have
time for neither . . . We are happy . . . when their own race is
chosen . . . their own class reaffirmed . . . their own desire sub-
merged . . . into   food . . . dishes . . . laundry . . . babies . . . no
dreams this week thank you I haven't the time . . . Like over-
ripe fruit in an orchard embraced by frost . . . the will to live
turns rotten . . . feckless . . . feculent . . .

What is a woman . . . to think . . . when all she hears . . . are
words that exclude her . . . all she feels . . . are emotions that
deceive . . . What do the children think . . . in their evening
quest . . . of those who from platform and pulpit . . . deride
their condition . . . yet purchase their service . . . What must
life be . . . to any young captive . . . of its time . . . Do we send
them back . . . home to the remembered horrors . . . Do we
allow them their elsewheres . . . to parade their talents . . . Do
we pretend that all is well . . . that Ends . . .

# Charles White

The art of Charles White is like making love
in the early evening
after the cabs have stopped
to pick you up and the doorman said
"Good evening ma'am. Pleasant weather we're having"

The images of Charles White remind me
of eating cotton candy at the zoo on a rainy day
and the candy not melting and all the other kids wondering
why

I remember once when I was little
before I smoked too many cigarettes
entering the church picnic sack race
I never expected to win just thought it would be fun
I came in second and drank at least a gallon
of lemonade then wandered off
to an old rope swing

Of all the losses of modern life the swing
in the back yard is my special regret
one dreams going back and forth of time and space
stopping bowing to one's sheer magnificence
pumping higher and higher space blurs time
and the world stops spinning while I in my swing
give a curtsey correctly
my pigtails in place and my bangs cut
just right

"But why aren't the artists the politicians" she asked
"because they're too nice" was the reply
"too logical too compassionate"
which not understanding I took to mean "sexy"—at least
that's how come and passionate were used in the novels
Johnetta and I used to sneak and read

And in the grown up world I think I understand
that passion is politics that being is beauty
and we are all in some measure responsible
for the life we live and the world
we live in

Some of us take the air, the land, the sun
and misuse our spirits     others of us have earned
our right to be called men and women

Charles White and his art were introduced to me
through magazines and books—that's why I love them

Charles White and his art were shared with me through
love and concern—that's why I value those

Charles White and his art live in my heart and the heart
of our people—that's why I think
love is worthwhile

# The Drum

*(for Martin Luther King, Jr.)*

The drums . . . Pa-Rum . . . the rat-tat-tat . . . of drums . . .
The Pied Piper . . . after leading the rats . . . to death . . . took
the children . . . to dreams . . . Pa-Rum Pa-Rum . . .

The big bass drums . . . the kettles roar . . . the sound of an-
imal flesh . . . resounding against the wood . . . Pa-Rum Pa-
Rum . . .

Kunta Kinte was making a drum . . . when he was captured
. . . Pa-Rum . . .
Thoreau listened . . . to a different drum . . . rat-tat-tat-Pa-
Rum . . .
King said just say . . . I was a Drum Major . . . for peace . . .
Pa-Rum Pa-Rum . . . rat-tat-tat Pa-rum . . .

Drums of triumph . . . Drums of pain . . . Drums of life . . .
Funeral drums . . . Marching drums . . . Drums that call . . .
Pa-Rum Pa-Rum . . . the Drums that call . . . rat-tat-tat-tat . . .
the Drums are calling . . . Pa-Rum Pa- Rum . . . rat-tat-tat Pa-
Rum . . .

# A Poem on the Assassination of Robert F. Kennedy

Trees are never felled . . . in summer . . . Not when the fruit . . . is yet to be borne . . . Never before the promise . . . is fulfilled . . . Not when their cooling shade . . . has yet to comfort . . .

But there are those . . . unheeding of nature . . . indifferent to ecology . . . ignorant of need . . . who . . . with ax and sharpened saw . . . would . . . in boots . . . step forth damaging . . .

Not the tree . . . for it falls . . . But those who would . . . in summer's heat . . . or winter's cold . . . contemplate . . . the beauty . . .

# Eagles
(a Poem for Lisa)

Eagles are a majestic species . . . living in the thin searing air
. . . building
nests on precipitous ledges . . .
    they are endangered . . . but unafraid . . .

An eagle's nest is an inverted dimple . . . made of ready smiles
. . . unbleached
saris . . . available arms . . . and clean soap smells . . .
    to withstand all . . . elements . . .

Nestled in the chocolate chaos . . . destined to become:
        roller skaters
        submarine eaters
        telephone talkers
        people
    are improperly imprinted ducklings . . .

Eagles perched . . . on those precipitous ledges . . . insist upon
teaching . . .
    the young . . . to fly . . .

# Her Cruising Car
*A Portrait of Two Small Town Girls*

There is nothing ... that can be said ... that can frighten me ... anymore ... Sadden me ... perhaps ... disgust me ... certainly ... but not make me afraid ... It has been said ... Learn What You Fear ... Then Make Love To It ... dance with it ... put it on your dresser ... and kiss it good ... night ... Say it ... over and over ... until in the darkest hour ... from the deepest sleep ... you can be awakened ... to say Yes ...

She never learned ... no matter how often people tried ... that it was hers ... the fear and the Life ... the glory of the gamble ... It was her quarter ... she had to pick the machine ... She never understood ... simple duty ... knowing only to give all of herself ... or none ... There was no balance ... to her triangle ... though three points ... are the strongest mathematical figures ... no tingle ... when struck ... no joy ... in her song ... no comfort in her chair ... war/always war ... with who she was ... who she wanted to be ... and what they wanted ... of her ...

One reason I think ... I am qualified ... to run the world ... though my appointment is not imminent ... is when I get ... what I want ... I am happy ... It is surprising to me ... how few people are ... When they win ... like Richard Nixon or John McEnroe ... they are unhappy ... when they lose ... impossible ... One reason I think ... I have neither ulcers nor nail biting habits ... is I know to be careful ... of what I want ... I just may get it ...

She was never taught ... that everything is earned ... that Newton was right ... for every action there is an equal and opposite reaction ... Interest is obtained ... only on Savings ... Personality is developed ... only on risk ... What is sought ... must first be given ... We please others ... by only allowing them access ... to that part of ourselves which is public ... If familiarity breeds contempt ... use breeds hatred ...

Turtles ... the kind you find in pet stores ... the kind Darwin met on Galápagos ... grow to fit the environment ... There are ... probably ... some genetic limits ... but a small turtle ... in a small bowl ... will not outgrow ... her home ... Flowers ... will rise ... proportionate more to the size ... of the pot ... than the relationship of sun ... to rain ... Humans seldom deviate ... If she hadn't been a small town girl ... with a mind and heart molded absolutely ... to fit the environment ... she might have developed ... a real skill ... a real desire ... to discover herself ... and her gifts ... As it was ... as it is ... she simply got used ... and used to using ...

She was never a loner ... never made ... to understand that life ... in fact ... is a solitary journey ... that only *one* ... was going to St. Ives ... that **no** one held her bag ... while the old woman traveled to Skookum ... that the Little Red Hen and the Engine That Could ... did it themselves ... She was ... let's face it ... the leader of the pack ... the top of the heap ... cheerleader extraordinaire ... She was very popular ... sought after by all the right people ... for her jokes ... her parties ... her parents' car ... The telephone was invented ... just for her ... She set up the friendships ... the going steadys ... the class officers ... yearbook staff ... Who's-In-Who's- Out ... through the witch wire ... Nothing could happen ... without her input ... She actually thought ... it was important ... who went with whom ... to the junior prom ... But somebody had to pick up the fallen streamers ... sweep the now scarred dance floor ... turn out the lights before they could go home ...

We were born ... in the same year ... our mothers delivered ... by the same doctor ... of the same city ... in the same hospital . . . We were little chubby girls in pink . . . passing cigarettes at the lawn parties . . . My mother made me play . . . with her . . . and hers . . . with me . . . We didn't really mind . . . we shared the same friends . . . hers . . . and the same ideas . . . mine . . . Maybe I became . . . too accustomed . . . to the sameness . . . It was certainly easier . . . for me to shed . . . her friends . . . than she to shed . . . my notions . . . Our mothers belonged . . . to the same clubs . . . Our fathers tracked . . . the same night devils . . . They all had the same expectations . . . from . . . of . . . at . . . or to . . . us . . . I liked to brood . . . she didn't . . . She liked to laugh . . . I didn't . . . I thought I was ugly . . . she didn't . . .

Pots are taught not to call kettles Black . . . people who live in glass houses . . . don't throw stones . . . small town girls learn early . . . or not at all . . . that they can make a life . . . or abort the promise . . . One of us tried . . . one of us didn't have to . . . To each . . . according to her birth . . . from each according to her ability . . . Which is bastardized Marx . . . but legitimate bourgeoisie . . . She was never caring . . . She never learned to see . . . beyond her own windshield . . . that there were other people on the sidewalk . . . other cars . . . on the road . . . She drank . . . too much . . . for too long . . . Maybe in the back of her mind . . . or heart . . . or closet . . . there was a sign saying: There-Is-More-Than-This . . . but she wouldn't pull it out . . . put it up . . . or even acknowledge that some things . . . many things . . . were missing . . . I accept . . . if not embrace . . . the pain . . . the sign on my car says: I Brake For Gnomes . . . the one in my heart reads: Error In Process— Please Send Chocolate . . .

Into the rising sun . . . or setting years . . . accustomed to the scattered friends littering the road . . . she drives on . . . with the confidence of small town drivers who know every wayfall . . . toward the smaller minds . . . around the once hopeful

lovers ... into the illusion of what it is ... to be a woman ...
through the delusion that trip necessitates ... never once
slowing ... to ask Did I Hurt You ... May I Love You ...
Can I/May I Please Give ... You A Lift ... With the surety
... of one who never had to walk ... she accelerates ...
toward boredom ... secure in the understanding ... that
everybody knows her ... and would be unlikely to ticket ...
her cruising car ... She was my friend ... more than a sister
... really ... a part of the mirror ... against which I adjust ...
my makeup ... I have no directions ... but here is a sign ...
Thomas Wolfe was wrong ... Maybe it will be read ...

# Harvest

*(for Rosa Parks)*

There is an old story . . . I learned in church . . . one evening . . . about a preacher . . . and his deacon . . . fishing . . . It seems that every time . . . the good brother got a bite . . . the fish would scamper . . . away . . . and the deacon . . . would curse . . . The preacher . . . probably feeling . . . his profession demanded . . . a response . . . said to the deacon Brother . . . should you curse like that . . . with me here . . . over some fish . . . And the deacon agreed . . . They fished on . . . the deacon losing more fish . . . when finally a big big one . . . got away . . . The deacon remembered his vow . . . looked at his empty pole . . . reminded himself of the vow . . . looked at his empty pole . . . sucked in his breath . . . turned to the preacher . . . and remarked Reverend . . . Something Needs To Be Said . . .

I guess everybody wants . . . to be special . . . and pretty . . . the boys . . . just want to be strong . . . or fast . . . all the same things . . . children want . . . everywhere . . . It was ordinary . . . as far as I can see . . . my childhood . . . but . . . well . . . I don't know . . . much . . . about psychology . . . We had a lot of pride . . . growing up . . . in Tuskegee . . . You could easily see . . . what our people could do . . . if somebody set a mind . . . to it . . . Father was a carpenter . . . Mama taught school . . . I got married . . . at nineteen . . .

You always felt . . . you should do something . . . It just wasn't right . . . what they did to Negroes . . . and why Negroes . . . let it happen . . . Colored people couldn't vote . . . couldn't use the bathroom in public places . . . couldn't go to the same library they paid taxes for . . . had to sit on the back of the buses . . . couldn't live places . . . work places . . . go to movies . . . amusement parks . . . Nothing . . . if you were colored . . . Just signs . . . always signs . . . saying No . . . No . . . No . . . My husband is a fine man . . . a fighting man . . . When we were young . . . belonging to the N double A C P was radical . . . dangerous . . . People got killed . . . run out of town . . . beaten and burned out . . . just for belonging . . . My husband belonged . . . and I belonged . . . In 1943 . . . during the war . . . Double Victory was just as important . . . one thing without the other was not good . . . enough . . . I was elected Secretary . . . of the Montgomery branch . . . I am proud . . . of that . . . Many people think History . . . just fell on my shoulders . . . or at my feet . . . 1 december 1955 . . . but that's not true . . .

Sometimes it seemed it was never going . . . to stop . . . That same driver . . . who had me arrested . . . had put me off a bus . . . from Maxwell Air Base . . . where I had worked . . . or maybe they all . . . look the same . . . I wasn't looking . . . for anything . . . That Colvin girl had been arrested . . . and nobody did anything . . . I didn't think . . . they would do anything . . . when the driver told us . . . it was four of us . . . to move . . . Three people moved . . . I didn't . . . I couldn't . . . it was just so . . . wrong . . . Nobody offered to go . . . with me . . . A neighbor . . . on the same bus . . . didn't even tell . . . my husband . . . what had happened . . . I just thought . . . we should let them know . . . *I* should let them know . . . it wasn't right . . . You have to realize . . . I was forty years old . . . all my life . . . all I'd seen . . . were signs . . . that everything was getting worse . . .

The press people came . . . around after . . . we won . . . I had to reenact . . . everything . . . I was on the aisle . . . the man by the window . . . got up . . . I don't fault him . . . for getting up . . . he was just doing . . . what he was told . . . Across the aisle were two women . . . they got up . . . too . . . There was a lot of violence . . . physical and verbal . . . I kinda thought . . . something might happen . . . to me . . . I just didn't . . . couldn't . . . get up . . .

They always tell us one . . . person doesn't make any difference . . . but it seems to me . . . something . . . should be done . . . In all these years . . . it's strange . . . but maybe not . . . nobody asks . . . about my life . . . If I have children . . . why I moved to Detroit . . . what I think . . . about what we tried . . . to do . . . somehow . . . you want to say things . . . are better . . . somehow . . . they are . . . not in many ways . . . People . . . older people . . . are afraid . . . younger people . . . are too . . . I really don't know . . . where it will end . . . Our people . . . can break . . . your heart . . . so can other . . . people . . . I just think . . . it makes a difference . . . what one person does . . . young people forget that . . . what one person does . . . makes a difference . . .

The deacon . . . of course . . . wanted to curse . . . because the fish got . . . away . . . perhaps there is something . . . other to be done . . . about the people we lose . . . We always talk . . . about how everyone was Black . . . before it was fashionable . . . overlooking the reality . . . that were that true . . . Black would have been fashionable . . . before it was . . . and might have stayed in vogue . . . longer than it did . . . Something needs to be said . . . about Rosa Parks . . . other than her feet . . . were tired . . . Lots of people . . . on that bus . . . and many before . . . and since . . . had tired feet . . . lots of people . . . still do . . . they just don't know . . . where to plant them . . .

# Sky Diving

I hang on the edge
    of this universe
    singing off-key
    talking too loud
    embracing myself
    to cushion the fall

I shall tumble
    into deep space
    never in this form
    or with this feeling
    to return to earth

    It is not tragic

I will spiral
    through that Black hole
    losing skin     limbs
        internal organs
    searing
    my naked soul

Landing
    in the next galaxy
    with only my essence
    embracing myself
    as

I dream of you

## A Journey

It's a journey ... that I propose ... I am not the guide ... nor technical assistant ... I will be your fellow passenger ...

Though the rail has been ridden ... winter clouds cover ... autumn's exuberant quilt ... we must provide our own guideposts ...

I have heard ... from previous visitors ... the road washes out sometimes ... and passengers are compelled ... to continue groping ... or turn back ... I am not afraid ...

I am not afraid ... of rough spots ... or lonely times ... I don't fear ... the success of this endeavor ... I am Ra ... in a space ... not to be discovered ... but invented ...

I promise you nothing ... I accept your promise ... of the same we are simply riding ... a wave ... that may carry ... or crash ...

It's a journey ... and I want ... to go ...

# Resignation

I love you
    because the Earth turns round the sun
    because the North wind blows north
        sometimes
    because the Pope is Catholic
        and most Rabbis Jewish
    because winters flow into springs
        and the air clears after a storm
    because only my love for you
        despite the charms of gravity
        keeps me from falling off this Earth
        into another dimension
I love you
    because it is the natural order of things

I love you
    like the habit I picked up in college
        of sleeping through lectures
        or saying I'm sorry
        when I get stopped for speeding
    because I drink a glass of water
        in the morning
        and chain-smoke cigarettes
        all through the day
    because I take my coffee Black
        and my milk with chocolate
    because you keep my feet warm
        though my life a mess
I love you
    because I don't want it
        any other way

I am helpless
    in my love for you

It makes me so happy
    to hear you call my name
I am amazed you can resist
    locking me in an echo chamber
    where your voice reverberates
    through the four walls
    sending me into spasmatic ecstasy
I love you
    because it's been so good
    for so long
    that if I didn't love you
    I'd have to be born again
    and that is not a theological statement
I am pitiful in my love for you


The Dells tell me Love
    is so simple
    the thought though of you
    sends indescribably delicious multitudinous
    thrills throughout and through-in my body
I love you
    because no two snowflakes are alike
    and it is possible
    if you stand tippy-toe
    to walk between the raindrops
I love you
    because I am afraid of the dark
        and can't sleep in the light
    because I rub my eyes
        when I wake up in the morning
        and find you there
    because you with all your magic powers were
        determined that
I should love you
    because there was nothing for you but that

I would love you
I love you
    because you made me
        want to love you
    more than I love my privacy
        my freedom     my commitments
          and responsibilities
I love you 'cause I changed my life
    to love you
    because you saw me one friday
        afternoon and decided that I would
love you
I love you I love you I love you

# I Wrote a Good Omelet

I wrote a good omelet...and ate a hot poem...
after loving you

Buttoned my car...and drove my coat home...in the
    rain...
after loving you

I goed on red...and stopped on green...floating
    somewhere in between...
being here and being there...
after loving you

I rolled my bed...turned down my hair...slightly
    confused but...I don't care...
Laid out my teeth...and gargled my gown...then I stood
    ...and laid me down...
to sleep...
after loving you

# Three/Quarters Time

Dance with me . . . dance with me . . . we are the song . . . we
are the music . . .
Dance with me . . .

Waltz me . . . twirl me . . . do-si-do please . . . peppermint
twist me . . . philly
Squeeze

Cha cha cha . . . tango . . . two step too . . .
Cakewalk . . . charleston . . . bougaloo . . .

Dance with me . . . dance with me . . . all night long . . .
We are the music . . . we are the song . . .

# Cancers

*(not necessarily a love poem)*

Cancers are a serious condition . . . attacking internal organs
   . . . eating
them away . . . or clumping lumps . . . together . . .

The blood vessels carry . . . cancerous cells . . . to all body
   parts . . . cruising
would be the term . . . but this is not necessarily a love
   poem . . .

Cancer is caused . . . by . . .
      the air we breathe
      the food we eat
      the water we drink
Indices are unusually high . . . in cities that have baseball
   teams
. . . or people . . .

      Coffee . . . milk . . . saccharine
      cigarettes . . . sun . . . and birth control
      devices . . .
are among the chief offenders . . .
      Monthly phenomena stopped . . . internally . . . will
         only lead . . .
      to shock syndrome . . .
What indeed . . . porcelana . . . does a woman . . . want . . .
Cancers are . . .
      the new plague
      the modern black death
      all that is unknown
         yet

I have a cancer . . . in my heart . . . I'm told . . . on
    knowledgeable authority . . .
it is not possible
For the heart we have . . .
        cardiac arrest . . . and outright attacks . . .
        holes in valves . . . and valve stoppage . . .
        constricted vessels . . . and nefarious air
            bubbles . . .

But then . . . my doctor never saw you . . . and doesn't
    believe
. . . in the zodiac . . .

# I Am She
**For Nancy**

I am she . . . making rainbows . . . in coffee cups . . . watching fish jump . . . after midnight . . . in my dreams . . .

On the stove . . . left front burner . . . is the stew . . . already chewed . . . certain to burn . . . as I dream . . . of waves . . . of nothingness . . .

Floating to shore . . . riding a low moon . . . on a slow cloud . . . I am she . . . who writes . . . the poems . . .

## You Were Gone

You were gone
    like a fly lighting
    on that wall
    with a spider in the corner
You were gone
    like last week's paycheck
    for this week's bills
You were gone
    like the years between
    twenty-five and thirty
    as if somehow
You never existed
    and if it wouldn't be
    for the gray hairs
    I'd never know that
You had come

Occasional

# Poem:

*A Poem for*

# langston
# hughes

# A Poem
### for langston hughes

diamonds are mined . . . oil is discovered
gold is found . . . but thoughts are uncovered

wool is sheared . . . silk is spun
weaving is hard . . . but words are fun

highways span . . . bridges connect
country roads ramble . . . but i suspect

    if i took a rainbow ride
    i could be there by your side

metaphor has its point of view
allusion and illusion . . . too

meter . . . verse . . . classical . . . free
poems are what you do to me

let's look at this one more time
since i've put this rap to rhyme

    when i take my rainbow ride
    you'll be right there at my side

hey bop hey bop hey re re bop

Occasional

# Poem:

*But Since You*

# Finally Asked

*(A Poem*
*Commemorating*
*the 10th Anniversary*
*of the*
*Slave Memorial*
*at Mount Vernon)*

# But Since You Finally Asked

*(A Poem Commemorating the 10th Anniversary of the Slave Memorial at Mount Vernon)*

No one asked us . . . what we thought of Jamestown . . . in 1619 . . . they didn't even say . . . "Welcome" . . . "You're Home" . . . or even a pitiful . . . "I'm Sorry . . . But We Just Can't Make It . . . Without You" . . . No . . . No one said a word . . . They just snatched our drums . . . separated us by language and gender . . . and put us on blocks . . . where our beauty . . . like our dignity . . . was ignored

No one said a word . . . in 1776 . . . to us about Freedom . . . The rebels wouldn't pretend . . . the British lied . . . We kept to a space . . . where we owned our souls . . . since we understood . . . another century would pass . . . before we owned our bodies . . . But we raised our voices . . . in a mighty cry . . . to the Heavens above . . . for the strength to endure

No one says . . . "What I like about your people" . . . then ticks off the wonder of the wonderful things . . . we've given . . . Our song to God, Our strength to the Earth . . . Our unfailing belief in forgiveness . . . I know what I like about us . . . is that we let no one turn us around . . . not then . . . not now . . . we plant our feet . . . on higher ground . . . I like who we were . . . and who we are . . . and since someone has asked . . . let me say: I am proud to be a Black American . . . I am proud that my people labored honestly . . . with forbearance and dignity . . . I am proud that we believe . . . as no other people do . . . that all are equal in His sight . . . We didn't write a constitution . . . we live one . . . We didn't say "We the People" . . . we are one . . . We didn't have to add . . . as an after-thought . . . "Under God" . . . We turn our faces to the rising sun . . . knowing . . . a New Day . . . is always . . . beginning

# Title Index

# First Line Index